Advance Praise

"Christine's impassioned, mindful and encouraging words hearten one to work beyond betrayal. By sharing her personal story of betrayal, we are gently guided on a path to self-acceptance. A path away from being the victim to one of self-validation." – Mary P.W.

"In reading this book, I started with a journey into finding the answers about betrayal. However, I ended up with the most important thing in life finding "BigLove". Thank you, Christine, for sharing your process and wisdom with all your sister warriors. With all my love." – Cia M.0

"I wish I had this book to read years ago. It probably wouldn't have impacted the final outcome of my marriage, but it would have helped me get through all the things, the author Christine, so thoroughly and thoughtfully touches on. There is so much of value in this book! It's even relative to me now, years after my divorce. As Christine says, learn to love yourself. Forgiveness is the key to living again." – Theresa K.

"The book *Roots of Forgiveness* is beautifully written by Chris. I have not personally experienced the affair of a partner, but I certainly have been betrayed. I know the pain and anguish that goes hand in hand with the act of betrayal. Chris addresses the disabling pain, the decision to stay or leave, and the choices we all face in the midst of such a situation. This memoir style book showed me the magic and miracles of forgiveness. In choosing forgiveness I see that I can experience a big love that moves me to fully embrace my personal wholeness and worth. And from that place, all of my life become bigger and better. Thank you, Chris, for sharing your journey and for showing me how to courageously use forgiveness to create a life filled with peace, hope, love and joy." – Lisa W.

"If you find yourself at the crossroads of betrayal and dishonesty, this book provides you a roadmap to recovery. Christine's resilience and loving responses offer often overlooked solutions to difficult problems. A worthwhile read." – Linda P.

"This book takes you through each segment of a painful journey, applying tools for growth, self-awareness, and understanding along the way. Christine offers validation for every emotional aspect that impacts those who experience betrayal and paves a path to recovery." – Kelly M.

"A wonderful book for those who are struggling with betrayal and forgiveness in their lives. It will help you explore hurt from the past and gently guide you to self-awareness and positive change for the future. An engaging, heartfelt and beneficial read." – Marn F.

"With *Roots of Forgiveness,* Christine Leon presents us with a unique and immensely rewarding guide through one of the most difficult of human processes. By applying her essential elements, readers can reach past pain and bitterness through to tangible healing. She provides a clear azimuth for women past the damage to a better and more powerful relationship, while unloading negative emotions along the way. Additionally, this work is a valuable guide to all men seeking to understand the forgiveness process and discover their role in it. A singularly superb work." – Fargoe T. G.

roots *of* forgiveness

roots *of* forgiveness

Find Freedom to Heal in Your Marriage After Betrayal

CHRISTINE ELIZABETH LEON

NEW YORK

LONDON • NASHVILLE • MELBOURNE • VANCOUVER

roots *of* forgiveness

Find Freedom to Heal in Your Marriage After Betrayal

Published in New York, New York, by Morgan James Publishing in partnership with Difference Press. Morgan James is a trademark of Morgan James, LLC. www.MorganJamesPublishing.com

ISBN 9781642794717 paperback
ISBN 9781642794724 eBook
ISBN 9781642795264 audiobook
Library of Congress Control Number: 2019901296

Cover & Interior Design by:
Christopher Kirk
www.GFSstudio.com

Morgan James is a proud partner of Habitat for Humanity Peninsula and Greater Williamsburg. Partners in building since 2006.

Get involved today! Visit
MorganJamesPublishing.com/giving-back

For my sons, Lucas and Josh – You are my Sun, Stars and Moon.
For my grandson, Archer Mays – You are my Love Bug Super Hero
&
For "my guy," whose courageous Heart I carry with me, in my
Heart – You are my Beloved.

Table of Contents

Your Love Letter xiii

Chapter 1: The Train That Hit Me 1

Chapter 2: Eight Essential Elements to Transformational
Healing Beyond Betrayal 15

Chapter 3: Grief is Your Source of Grace 23

Chapter 4: Your Essence of Love – BigLove 49

Chapter 5: Your Rooted Queendom of Fierce Forgiveness .67

Chapter 6: U R Awesome 83

Chapter 7: Your Magical Unicorn Perspective 95

Chapter 8: Showing Up for Yourself 105

Chapter 9: Your Heart Warrior Bootcamp 119

Chapter 10: Your Heroine's Journey 139

Chapter 11: Invitations for Practice 147

Chapter 12: Once Upon A Time to Begin Again 151

Missing You – A Poem 155

A Little Parable for You 159

End Notes and References 161

Acknowledgments 165
About the Author 171
Thank You!. 175

Your Love Letter

As I began writing this love letter for you, I tried to remember the first thing I wanted to hear, in those first pages, in the many books I opened – when I was where you are now. What answers did my heart most need to hear? So that I might intuitively sense what your heart is searching to hear now.

You might want to hear that there is an end to the nightmare of your awake life now. That there is a way, a formula, a fix, or someone who can stop the intense full-body heartache that you are walking-wounded with every second of every minute since "the event" happened. The event, as we know, is that time-stopping instant of the phone call, the text message, the email, the note, the hotel key, the ticket stub, the credit card bill, the overheard whisper, the Facebook thread, the photos, or the actual sighting – when the explosion happened.

Whatever the vehicle of revelation, that sudden unexpected moment of stark exposure which opened your eyes, zap-shocked your body, stopped your breath and broke your heart wide open – is the "event." The painful electrocution that surged through you at the thought that someone else was with him, touched him, received his smile, hugged him, and captured his attention. Took him away from you. It could have been for one afternoon, or it might have been for three or more secretive years. What matters is you. The wounded egoic thoughts that now haunt your tender psyche, like an uninvited magpie squawking, "you were fooled, you were deceived, you were cheated-on, he betrayed you!"

To name it - the "event"- is a trick I used for myself in the beginning to put a little space between the feelings that come up when saying the word "affair." It's not denial. It is a self-compassionate trick that I found was useful until I had some muscles under my belt with which to hold the raw truth in my hands. Choose for yourself in naming the event, but, be mindful that words are powerful energy. My trick worked for me on my path to healing, so use my choice with love or find your own self-compassionate trick. Either way, there is no escaping the reality of this massive shift.

The "event", coldly defined is this: Your husband had an affair. Your husband, the man you love, the love of your life, the partner you trust, your best friend – has betrayed you. Suddenly a state of sadness, anger, outrage, disappointment wash over you as you realize you have just been hit by a train. Only you didn't physically die. Standing in an emotional and physical shock, you sense something has died. It feels like death. Like pain pouring down on you, your skin heats up, your eyes sting with tears, and your throat squeezes off your swallow as you're blasted from your comfort zone into a frighteningly surreal reality, which is that your world has just been crashed into by betrayal. In that second, your universe literally explodes.

Paralyzed, numbing tears fall as your first panicky thoughts form: "What do I do now?" Then your second: "This can't be true." Then, rapid-fire: "I know him." "Or do I?" *"Who is he?"* And, for many women the next thoughts are: "I feel like I could kill him!" Or, "I wish he would die!"

Now, darling, stay with me; maybe you have had those thoughts, maybe not. Still, as scary and hard-hearted as they might sound, having these thoughts is normal. However, acting on them is irreversibly criminal and not a step toward healing for anyone. It is a precious price too high to pay. Rest assured, within this journey, you will find freedom to heal those thoughts, as well.

What is worthy of attention is your awareness of the profound toll the pain of betrayal can heap upon you, which can open up your potential to become someone who thinks, acts, and speaks in a manner even you may not recognize. During those first days, absent a brave self-control that affords you the choice of how to show up in this sudden onset of pain, there is a rage and revenge power-storm swirling in you that could possibly create destruction beyond even your understanding.

Some wounded hearts have shared that their rage storms produced phone calls to their husband's bosses to report the interloping co-worker. While blinded by rage to the possible consequences for her and her family, punishing the offending husband's source of income and reputation through edgy exposure seemed a good idea. Her defensive reflex ignited from the core of her profound pain and triggered a destructive motion with potential to ripple back upon her regardless of whether she stayed or left.

Another story from the field of wounded hearts was of a woman in a financially wealthy marriage. The choice she made with her husband, after discovery of his betrayal, was to stay and forgive him. However, her real goal was to feign forgiveness only to strategically take as much as she could from the marriage, to punish him, before she left him for good. Chances are good she was a wonderful and gentle woman before being betrayed, and not knowing where to turn, what to do, or how to end her pain, simply ate that person up.

To get stuck in this state of Being is a path to eating oneself alive. The emotional impact of the event has the capability to transform us into someone-else in the eye of this hurricane. It's a little like shape-shifting in movies about aliens. The beauty of this awareness is that we each have the power to pull ourselves back from going to the dark side. We just need to want to. We do have a choice.

These precious vulnerable women, whose stories were shared here illustrate our fragility in relationship, and each responded through their deepest urge of agonizing pain. They cried out from heartbroken rage with a behavior that even they did not think could come from them. It happens. While we are still whole, we observe and think we would never respond like this. But not so fast. The depth from which our primal outcry rises, like mercury in a thermostat rushing up and out of us, is a shock to us, as well. Those of us inside, up-close and personal, witnessing other's pain, are called to offer loving compassion, understanding, and support, without judgment. We never know what we will truly do till we are standing in those shoes.

Some women find a way to stay in their marriage and *will* themselves, stiff upper lip and all, to get past it. They accept that the wound will simply lie dormant like a bad dream buried and forgotten. From then on, they simply hope that nothing digs it up. Some simply deny and suppress. It didn't happen. Or, oh that's old history. We're past that. Three hushed monkeys side-by-side. See no evil, hear no evil, speak no evil. It did not happen.

Well, dear friend, that's not the way I see for you. My wish is that you find my love letter to you and its promise that there is a powerful and positive path forward, and that you will choose to begin your journey on this healing path from wherever you are now.

Your truth is that this was the very last thing you ever expected. You did everything for him. Or maybe you were always a little worried about everything. You had such a busy schedule, you "shoulda, coulda, woulda" given more time, paid more attention – you were "gonna", as soon as the big pressing "thing" was done. Or: You had an intuitive inkling, in the back of your mind, but never really paid attention to it. You trusted him. He suddenly seemed happier and it was great. You just thought that it was a good thing.

Darling. It doesn't matter. The event is real; it happened. It is excruciatingly painful, it is "overwhelmingly" overwhelming, and most important to note – it is not your fault.

You have unexpectedly been torn from your life as you knew it and thrown into an emotional burning heart-crash. There is no doubt about it, you have been traumatized. I know intimately what that feels like. The first thing my experience tells me is that what you want to hear from this book is wise and loving and kind support; a safe container in which to feel seen in your vulnerable injured state. You also want clear guidance with a promise that there is indeed a way to genuinely heal to the life and love you choose to have beyond the betrayal. In this book, my love letter to you, we will journey a path to genuine healing. But before we do let's go deeper into where you are and how you got there.

To begin, imagine holding your aching heart in a cradle of loving-kindness to create a little sacred space for this very courageous and vulnerable journey we will walk together. Sit back, relax, and be invited to breathe deeply from your highest possible place – your powerful heart. Profoundly wounded, yes. Dead, no. Trust me. Gently relax in your body and open it to deep slow breaths – best you can. I see you. You are no longer invisible. You no longer need to hide. You matter. You are not alone on this journey, and you are not alone in this crushing experience. Together, we will hold hands and walk forward to a different state of Being, to a stronger more empowered You. From the very wounded place where you are now, and on to where you want to grow, with all your heart. To a genuine healing within your marriage. My goal is to help you heal.

You might be saying this sounds like very "woo-woo" and "out-there flitty" stuff. You may think it's not grounded, scientific or practical sounding enough for you. That might feel true to you. However, dear friend, I offer you another truth to consider which my experience has proven to me. This healing path is the profound work of a Woman-Warrior, a Love Warrior, a Queen of her own Heart – which requires the calling-in of all the beautiful inherent super powers that live inside of You.

This journey will not be easy. As a matter of fact, it will be undeniably hard. These mysterious and magical things we call love and the dynamic of relationships, are made-up of complex human moving parts that can become very complicated and at times very messy. Therefore, the first thing you need to own before you start is a genuine commitment to your own healing. A commitment to recognize that you are not a victim. That you won't lay down or identify yourself as a victim. Instead, commit to see that you are a beautiful, brilliant, intelligent, sexy, desirable, fun, strong, loveable, fascinating woman – who simply forgot who she is, in the "day to day", of living her life. Who lost sight of her Self while singularly focused on the demanding managment of her amazing energy output for her family, work, and friends.

Who now has been shaken awake from her trance in the most brutal way possible.

Again, not your fault. It happened in a time when you were operating with comfortable confidence; intentionally giving your all to all from what you believed to be is the safe protected shelter of your marriage to your trusted husband. Indeed, it is the unexpected reckless handling of your heart, the rip of emotional abandonment, by the one you wholeheartedly counted on, the one you chose to spend the rest of your life with, who shook your foundation and reminded you that we are all vulnerable fallible Beings, and pain happens. You were living your life from trust. You didn't think you needed to be on watch. Which is the way most of us believe a good marriage should be. The promise of loyalty, safety and security is a part of the deal.

The deeper truth is this is not about blame – it is about the challenging dimensions of relationship. Your relationship with yourself, with your mate, and a new understanding that relationships are living breathing things, ever changing and challenging. Whether you already realized this valuable concept or not, it doesn't matter. You are here now, and I will lovingly continue to assure you that whatever your thoughts right now, this situation is not your fault.

What we will explore in these pages is a way to remember and rekindle the brilliance of *you* from your deepest energy of love, which in turn will ignite your healing power within your marriage. What is here is an awakening of self-empowerment for you from a compassionate awareness that there are a vast number of women in marriages or long-term relationships who have been betrayed and who have retreated out of shame, self-blame and fear into the shadows of silence. Shut off from conversations and friendship in fear of transparency because there is a painful secret she feels compelled to keep. Self-imprisoned to walk wounded every day with no one to lift her out of her cocoon of profound heartbreak because to tell is to be shamed. She stays in her marriage and settles for relationship crumbs that are offered by the one who broke her heart and who she lives in fear of leaving or being left by.

That is not living. That is a dead-heart walking. A lonely life sentence, and as I write this sentence, I send out a prayer, an intention, an invitation of love - for silent suffering hearts and to all wounded hearts of betrayal. That they will renew their search for healing paths and that they find for themselves in these pages their path to freedom.

Now, here is the really good news – you have discovered my love letter in this book written just for you. What is awesome is that you have seen yourself and courageously read this far and are still here. If you are, then a profoundly transformative opportunity has risen to the surface for you today. It is with your intention and desire to find a way to stay and heal the wound of betrayal in your marriage, you choose to open yourself to the life changing notion that you have initiated something extraordinary. It will require willingness to forgive and to be open to powerful new views, practices, and growth to get to the new life you want to create. Happiness – full range. Yes, to let in happiness again beyond betrayal, indeed, it is a tall order. The path holds many dimensions to be courageously peeled back and explored. That will require understanding, patience, clarity, faith and an openness to new ways of seeing things. Most importantly a loving and illuminating new way of seeing your Self.

These aspects and more will be among the heart seeds of personal power we will plant, inspire and nurture to grow. All are essential ingredients – if you are truly committed to igniting your healing. Oh, and one more thing, you will not be alone. I will be here on every level, in every element on this path with you in these pages. With my guiding words and planted intention for you, you will reach the healing place in you of peace, grace, love, and resilient strength.

Now, dear friend, take my offered hand, and let me show you the way out.

With Love.

Chapter 1:
The Train That Hit Me

"When you walk to the edge of all the light you have and take that first step into the darkness of the unknown, you must believe that one of two things will happen, there will be something solid to stand upon or you will be taught to fly."
– Patrick Overton

It was a Tuesday in February, late evening, almost three years ago. Out of the blue, a friend of mine called me up and asked me if I was aware of some *news?* I had no idea what she was referring to, but this simple question laid the track for my sudden plunge into a bad dream.

Before I go there, let me tell you a little about my guy and me.

You know those romantic and amazing stories of high school sweethearts? The couples who parted ways at graduation, lived their whole lives, and as destiny would have it, after twenty, thirty, forty or fifty years they circle back to discover each other again? Well, except for a few variations in the details, that's my story with my guy. In high school, we were secretly in young love with each other. So secretly, that neither ever told the other.

We were drawn to each other and made every nonchalant effort to spend time around each other, but both of us had complicated situations, insecurities, young limiting beliefs, and peer pressure that held us at bay, in this very small private-school social environment. Remember this was from inside the mind of two tender teenagers anxiously preparing to set out into the world.

During our three-year secret crush in high school and despite the brilliance of our combined young minds, we only found a way to have one date. We got up enough courage to invite each other to one formal dance. It turned out to be a dream night for us both. No, not the way you might think. We didn't kiss or do all things that more confident, young, opportunistic, and hormonally driven teens might do. We had the weight of Catholic taboos and reputation preservation pressure upon us. However, not even that was mighty enough to block the profound bonding that occurred between us on a human heart level that I can only describe as being with someone you were always meant to be with from the start. An undeniable feeling we both deeply and secretly felt. It was like coming home to your deepest sense of romantic love in a way you had never experienced. And it was so precious and pure. Still our youth and individual fears of unworthiness kept us from proclaiming what was there, and our silence seemingly communicated to each of us, that night, that we had gotten it wrong. So, we each dealt with the disappointment in our own way, while still claiming the willingness and desire to remain friends. As secretly painful as that was, we finished the school year grabbing sightings of each other from a bittersweet space and held onto the memories of the one romantic night. We stayed friends from a distance and packed away the dreams of what we wished could have been, and genuinely wished each other well into the future. Fast forward forty years.

The details around my life when my guy re-connected with me are for another book. However, suffice it to say, both he and I had done a lot of living. In the course of that forty years of living, in parallel and separate worlds – it was not surprising to find the presence of what relationship counselors might call "baggage". The unfinished or ongoing emotional aspects of prior relationships, life experiences, PTSD, children, and/or sometimes the drama "drag-out" that may, unfortunately, still accompany it. I'm not a fan of the term "baggage." My preference is to spell it out that, every relationship brings a life-marking experience that once left, requires attention, healing, and understanding to move on from, or it lies dormant and influences you, in one way or another, until you do. You can see that while "baggage" is simpler, I accept and enjoy being a wordy gal.

So, we rediscovered each other. Beginning with an exuberant delight for this reconnected friendship, we gradually realized the weight and volume of the complexities that our past brought forward. So we cautiously waded into the lake of romantic memories and unpacked what had lain dormant and unknown to the other. We still found, a profoundly attractive, magically vibrant, and knowing soul-song of us, bonded in that one night and carried with us like a tune you can't get out of your head, for those forty years. We shared our concerns about the "baggage" that we were bringing into our re-connection, but as we wrapped our confident hearts around each other within that stage of falling in love, of course we believed anything was manageable. So thus began, our present eight-year committed life partner relationship. At the time *my event* occurred, we were five and a half years in.

Rediscovering each other, for us, felt like a miracle. It is the acknowledgment of my miracle of love, with the tangible reality of how blessed and happy I felt, that I want to impress upon you as we move toward my retelling of the story of my devastating event.

Our first years reunited were very hard. Just back from the Middle East my guy took on a military training job in Death Valley, California, taken solely to be physically located together. Nine months into our relocation, his financial situation forced us to consider another job offer in the Middle East of a potential two to four-year span. Given his financial requirements, we agreed to weather the separation and committed to find ways to build and create a strong thriving relationship no matter what. To that end, I committed with intentional focus, to learn all things that developed my higher consciousness. I wanted to experience my self-empowerment growing, so that my core strength would build and be unshakeable for our challenge during this very hard period of unavoidable separation. With the fire of confidence that is felt in love and my juicy sense of joy, I set out to be more engaged with my life. I committed to discover my authentic calling. I knew I had something special to give, I just didn't know exactly what it was yet.

At the time, this quest for my calling was a giant, exciting adventure given that from a small child I was trained to believe that my role and responsibility was to be in service and self-sacrifice to others. In my family that was a given, and it translated into my young life, that my place of priority was behind everyone else. Take care of everyone else first. By the time my guy and I reconnected, I had realized my truth was something else.

Now an experienced adult, with a "Ph.D. in life", a recovered co-dependent with an actual degree in psychology, I wanted to identify my true strengths and gifts and find a way to love myself and be of service to others in a healthy, empowering, and productive way. It was then I decided to become a life and relationship coach. Inspired, I trained with a sense of higher life mission and completed courses with several coaching schools. Completing all the courses and officially certified, I was ready to begin building my practice.

I was on top of the world. The only thing that could be better was for my guy to complete his contract and come home. However, the contract kept coming up for extension, and the money seemed too good to pass on. There were too many obligations that he carried heavy responsibility for. After he had retired from the military, there were a lot of post-issues from his experiences in the military programs he was a central part of. He felt good having a job that made good money again. It brought him a sense of self-worth. I wanted that for him. I was willing to make the sacrifice till we could square all matters of our past, in a manner that felt good for us, and would bring us together on this side of the world.

As months passed, I had intuitive hits that some things didn't sound right. That his recall of things seemed a little off. His response to events or questions would light up a concern in me. Something seemed off. I didn't know what, and he was not open to being fished for answers, so I let it lie. I told myself that it was me reading into things and that I needed to trust him. To believe in him. I accepted that I had a choice and my choice was my power. I chose to believe in our love and his sincerity of love for me. We were friends, lovers, and destined life-partners. I chose to live that mutually proclaimed belief. Every day I woke with new intention to be stronger from love. I worked harder on myself. Our twice-daily Skype visits were more relaxed and lovingly engaged. After a few months passed, it seemed as though we had turned a corner. Our relationship seemed to root and build, and I felt we had finally reached a place of solid knowing, support, connection, understanding, and love. I believed that after all our enduring and dedicated relationship work, our individual growth of understanding, and vows of commitment, we had reached a point where we were doing and feeling genuinely solid and happy. I was certainly as happy as I could be, while we stayed focused on the future. It was a very loving and positive time.

Keep Your Arms Inside the Car

As I said at the beginning of the chapter, it was a late-night Tuesday in February. A Skype call chimed from my computer. I could see it was from my friend. She asked me if I had heard the news. I told her I had no idea what she was talking about. She told me about how she had seen a posting on Facebook by Wendy (*not her real name*) my guy's previous relationship, with whom he had produced a child. She was announcing that she was having IVF produced twins.

Not connecting any dots, I said that I was happy for her. "That's great!" I added.

My friend paused and asked, "Do you think he gave her any sperm for the babies?"

I told her, "Of course not. He would have talked to me about it."

Her eyes widened, her mouth pulled back, and she muttered, "O…K…" almost as though it was a question.

I held tight, and intentionally projected my absolute positive belief and trust that there was no way my guy, whom I had given everything to, did everything for, doted on every day for years – there was no way …. *no way* – he would do that to me.

My friend persisted, saying, "Well, I was just thinking maybe she and he froze sperm because they weren't exactly spring chickens during their relationship. It just made me think."

I smiled and forced myself to look relaxed on this Skype call with my well-intentioned friend. "What? I wouldn't think so," I continued. "But I will ask him on our call today."

And so I did. A little later, I called to put the question to him. "Did you know Wendy is pregnant? With IVF twins?"

Without skipping a beat, he replied, "How did you find out?"

"She posted an announcement on Facebook." I answered.

He quickly shot back, "I hate Facebook."

"I hate Facebook!" I thought. "Are you serious? I hate Facebook?" But while those were my thoughts, my mouth couldn't say a word, and I believe I went deaf too. The next thing that registered was him saying, "Listen, honey, I gotta go to work. I will call you after work. Okay?"

"Okay," I muttered. And he clicked off.

All night I sat with the hot anxiety of my racing thoughts. "What is he going to say?" "This can't be true!" "I'm sure it's not true!" "He didn't sound concerned." "Am I making too much of this?" I called in all my inner strength, meditation practice, good intentions, prayers and I may have also preformed some spells for good luck. All so that I might manage to control my *crazy*, cause crazy would do me no favors. It was bedtime, and I had to try to sleep. I set my alarm for the earliest time I could reach out to call him, after his workday. After all, his job was in the Middle East on the other side of the world. So, 5 a.m. I began trying to connect on Skype. Finally, he clicked on. He started out trying to do the easy and sweet hellos, the how are yous, but I would have nothing of it. Calmly I asked, "Did you give sperm to Wendy for those babies?"

"Yeah. That's what I wanted to talk to you about," he responded quickly.

In that exact moment –

Bam!

The train of betrayal crashed into me with fury and fierceness.

My journal entry, penned a few days later, says it best:

In that instant I felt my heart stop and break. A sense of overwhelming sadness, anger, disappointment filled my cells. Betrayal. The pain-filled vibrations of betrayal took over my Being. It was as though I suddenly had total amnesia about how feeling safe and loved had felt. As though that memory had just been brutally stripped away from me. This profound sadness has a surreal quality to it as it washes over me again and again. The more drenched I become, the more I uncontrollably sob. This is a No-Do-Over – like Death. This feels like death. My heart is broken wide open, shattered, and scattered. Like an explosion of me. All I can do is cry. There is no way to think your way out. Or to find the silver lining at this point – it is only to experience the waves of such pain of betrayal. In this one moment – I felt the loss of my best friend and love. The trust I had given him – is shattered beyond repair. I feel like a fool and a widow of love. Two babies – of my love's seed – to be produced for ultimate winnings by W. I feel like she has robbed me of something that belonged to me. Only me. I feel personally violated – helpless – because now the choice is so heavy and hard. Do I stay, or do I go?

Reality had come to hit me hard in the face. A fire-storm situation so unthinkable, so impossible to plan for and so pregnant with consequences for the future, had collided with my world. My guy was isolated in an extended contract situation. He lived in a manner that was frugal to the point of cargo box existence. Literally. His day consisted of Skypes with me and work. We made an extraordinary effort to build a genuine platform of support so that he could feel connected in our relationship. But years in any solitary living environment does funny things to a person. Add to that his suppressed missing of his little boy whom he dearly loves, whom he dreams of spending more time with and does everything he can to be sure he is cared for and safe. Now the match to light the firestorm: the broken personality of the child's mom. Book brilliant, street sharp, and singularly driven from a demonstrated core of narcissism mixed with the sociopathic absence of regard for others.

I blamed myself for this occurrence right along with my guy. I blamed my kindness and willingness to believe that if I sent her loving and kind intentions that she would be a different person. That good would come from it. I blamed myself for being so trusting and not forcing my way into interrogating every intuitive hit I had about things that seemed off. I blamed myself for being so dumb and trusting that he could stand up against her and protect me and protect us.

What I realized in hindsight was that her overall plan was to communicate to my guy her phony intention to have more kids or siblings separate of a parental partner. She expressed freedom from a need for financial or parental aid from a chosen sperm donor bank. She was ready to carry the load herself. She said their son needed siblings. In correspondence with me post-discovery, she referred to it all as the siblings project. She knew my guy's sense of responsibility, the vulnerability of his guilty nature, his impassioned love of children (especially since his military time in Iraq), and his protective self-sacrificing willingness to do whatever was necessary to protect his little child's world. What I was aware of, but felt was recently under control regarding his one child of their relationship, was her historically proven self-given permission to take boundless advantage of my guy. To freely demand, at her pleasure, as much financial support, as she wished. Her behavior demonstrated an outrageous entitlement to exploit his self-sacrificing generosity, vulnerability, and deep-rooted guilt. Gripping firmly, I grounded my effort to stay just this side of judgment, because I didn't walk in her shoes. I held intention to gather my perspective from her actual demonstration of how she chose to be, which proved her to be more covert than overt.

What I did learn from my guy was that their relationship was based in a mutual mission in a dangerous time and place. Such things happen in times of war-conflict. What held the relationship together was *not* enduring romantic love. Therefore, once out of that environmentally connecting influence their *incompatibility* was lit up. He had noted that in general before she gave birth, she exhibited behavior of one who didn't like or want kids. Pregnancy gave the appearance of changing her mind. What I ultimately came to realize was that her goal after the connecting circumstances passed was to focus on developing the perfect hook for a well-funded financial source of support for the rest of her days.

Once their relationship ended – her financial plan needed to be increased and locked-in. Regardless of her expressed acceptance and awareness of my invested relationship with my guy, she planned it out cold-heartedly. Knowing him and what would hook him, she worked her plan and manipulated him masterfully over a long period to a place of desperation, loss of sanity, and logic, until he voluntarily offered to give her sperm. Completely oblivious to the possible outcome of IVF multiple births, which could potentially imprison him financially for the rest of his third act of life, his main priority was protecting his little boy. He was convinced that the percent of chance for her success, at the door of fifty, was low enough for the gamble. He believed she might try but chances were good it wouldn't work. That she would tire of the process and move on from the idea. Most importantly, he believed above all that I would understand because I am me. He saw me as kind, loving, and giving, and to protect me, he didn't ask me. He believed *all* this from the isolation of his cargo box cell he lived in, alone, on the other side of the world.

The rest of the details are not relevant to this part of my sharing. What is relevant is that a hard reality fell heavy into my lap. The heartbreaking fact that now I had to decide about us – do I stay, or do I go? What criteria do I use to make a loving, and self-loving, decision? How do I know I can forgive him? How will I ever feel happy and normal again? Plus, there was no way around it, my heart was broken. How will I mend it, forgive, and not become a person on the same level of mean-spirit that Wendy has introduced to the game? Is forgiveness for this even possible? Whom can I tell that I can trust to be helpful and safe? How will I ever trust him again? Where do I start? How can I stop crying?

All of these and more questions looped through my head. I was a wreck beyond all wrecks. I felt a tremendous sense of depression overwhelming me and fear of the darkest dark that I felt in this place of no return. I thought about it for a good week. I cried uncontrollably for most of that time. I took all the pictures and reminders of my guy down, and I cleared my environment of everything that reminded me of the innocence of our love. I felt so betrayed that it was as though everything reminded me of my pain. I freed my eyes of anything that could remind me. It was like standing in front of a blank canvas.

I began to pull out all things spiritual: paints, brushes, supplies, books, poems, guides, prayers, and anything and everything that could be a source of guidance and higher power for any aspect of this huge very messy mess. I went to the mattresses, as they say in the *Godfather* movie. In this case, I went into myself on staycay retreat from everything and everyone until I could stop crying. So that I could engage in a thoughtful introspection of what I knew for sure and what I believed was possible.

Over the next few weeks, I slowly began my move forward. Stay or go decisions, but mostly how I would begin to put the pieces back together if I stayed. The journey was hard and long. Most of all, it required a willingness to forgive and heal. It took literally two and half years till I felt solidly back to the me of love that I am. During this, the logistical details surrounding my guy changed. He came home for good. The babies were born, their future is interwoven with our lives forever. Wendy is still difficult on many levels, but I believe anyone can evolve. Our plan is to remain committed and focused on our clear values and goals. No matter what.

The reason I wrote this love letter just for you; the reason I have made the choice to be vulnerable to judgment or criticism; to be courageously naked with my story, is because it took a lot of trial and error, hard personal work, arguing, and focused commitment to heal - that allowed me to find the answers. There were times I believed, even after my commitment to forgive, that the only answer was to end our relationship and move on.

This path to healing is very challenging. It will be as challenging for you and for your husband. As I said before, to genuinely heal beyond betrayal is the work of a woman with the "heart of a warrior." These are the women my clients are and that I believe I am. This is the ethos of my practice and it's the ethos of my love letter to you. My want for you is that you believe you can thrive with a love warrior's heart and build an unshakeable resilience for whatever comes in your life. For you to experience the benefit of what I believe with all my heart is a path of the elements to healing. The path I journeyed.

My mission is to bring this powerful love and support to you in these pages and beyond. I am not a doctor, but I do have a "Ph.D. in life" experience, the skills of a loving life coach, and the grateful peaceful whole heart of a woman in love with her guy again. The path I will share was created from my own journey to healing my relationship after betrayal, and beyond to happiness.

You have one decision in front of you: *Do you want to heal your pain?* Only with a willingness toward that can you begin exploring the courageous path to heal your relationship and yourself, beyond betrayal. Take my hand and let me introduce the essential elements of forgiveness that lit my way out of the dark hole.

Chapter 2:

Eight Essential Elements to Transformational Healing Beyond Betrayal

"When we are no longer able to change a situation, we are challenged to change ourselves."
– Viktor E. Frankl

My friend, most likely you have been called to my book for the following reasons. You have been betrayed by your closest love, you are in a state of heartbreak laced with threads of anger, and you believe to some degree that you want to stay in your marriage. The situation has brought to your door a Mt. Everest-size challenge. It's personal now. How you choose to show up is what will define the fabric of this experience of your life. I wrote this book for beauties like you who, in the heat of the fire, still desire to create something positive, strong, and enduring for themselves and their family. All they need is encouragement, a map, and wise support.

The eight elements you will train with represent the essential areas of deep personal work that my own experience has shown are required to ignite authentic healing for a wound so deep. The choice of areas named represent a path of trial and error on my quest to authentically heal my heart and relationship. I wanted what you want now. I tried each of these elements in a variety of usual ways. I practiced them with intention and a driving desire to heal. I even tried couple's counseling. Still, over time we seemed to grow further apart rather than closer. It was tangibly unbearable. We became sadder, or more hurt, or angrier, or self-righteous. At one point, I felt as though nothing would work. I began shifting to believe that ending and moving-on were our only hope to heal. I watched my tiring pattern surface, of getting lost, emoting, detaching, recalibrating, and coming back to re-engage. It began to get old. I began to feel old. Lucky for me, my cultivated fiery resilience pulled me back one more time, to stay curious, generous, courageous, and optimistic. It held open my last glimmer of willingness for deeper self-discovery, like a reluctant foot jammed in the door, long enough for a beautiful transformative breakthrough to occur.

The breakthrough I speak of is akin to the saying that someone is an overnight success. Actually, a closer look reveals that they had been working very hard on their craft to "make it" for ten or more years before they reached the "overnight' success.

These eight elements make-up the ingredients that brought healing to my experience, myself, and my relationship. The reality is that it took several years to understand how they work together. To feel and recognize the healing. My intention is to provide you guidance to clarity, direction, and support with more ease.

First upfront point for clarity is: the path is *forgiveness*. Forgiveness is love. Love is the mother ship for all the elements. Love is the way. Buddhist Monk Thich Nhat Hanh is known to have said, "There is no way to Happiness. Happiness is the way." While I believe this is true, I also believe we can just as easily plug in any of these words: love, forgiveness, joy, kindness, etc. Which widens our lens to the presence of a deeper universal Truth. The practice is the way. In these pages, I will share the way that I found.

The following chapters will highlight the essential layers for healing, of the many that exist, for each of the eight essential elements. With your fierce commitment to believe in the power of love, let us name love as our north star to keep us on track on this journey. We will dive deeply into the following topics in the eight elements: grief, love, forgiveness, power, perspective, self-care, developing your Being-muscles, and your special lens to see forward. We will unpack their qualities, graces and energies. Each will be presented as tools for your new toolbox as they relate to healing after betrayal. I am certain that the eight elements named are not new to you. However, I am confident that my perspective will bring something fresh and of empowering value to you. Illuminated in these chapters for your discovery, is a synergy of power and healing that is ignited from these elements working in partnership, that creates a foundation for healing.

This path will be challenging. I quite frequently would simply say to myself, "This is hard. Really hard." This level of personal work *is* hard. But, it is well worth the energy. You see, it is also the golden seed of a healing miracle blossoming in you that will unfold as it is meant to, for you. If you can't see it, have faith.

Before we start, here are some tips from the "experienced me". I am a trained life coach. I am an experienced woman of relationships. I am sixty-five years young. I have been on a quest for higher consciousness, authentic love and self-empowerment for decades starting earnestly in my forties. Still, I confess nothing prepared me for my experience. As I stumbled to find the way to healing, what I noticed most was that, as I began to feel better, I eased up on my awareness and practice. It is the same pattern many folks have with antibiotics. We feel better, we stop. My tip is don't stop. Stay steady and practice to increase your self-awareness each day. Stay open to engage with whatever supports you to bring your best to this daring experience. This is your life. Live it that way. Tenderly hold the intention to create extraordinary healing. Let us begin with a more detailed overview of what's to come.

Eight Essential Elements to Transformational Healing

Element One – Grace of Grief. This chapter on grief will cover its purpose, power, and meaning. How to grieve. What to grieve. How grief is your first self-compassionate and empowering step through it. The many faces of betrayal, the power it holds, and the way through it. How to see, understand, and engage depression to serve you. How to let go of the pain. Learn powerful practices to support you and inspire you to begin anew.

Element Two – Your Essence of Love - *BigLove*. This chapter is all things love. We will rediscover and reconnect to your deepest essence of love. Explore how love communicates to ignite forgiveness; how to communicate from love; how to center and embody love; and how the struggle itself is a gift. We will explore neuroplasticity, grace, boundaries, and deeply connecting with your Self. I will share the meaning and magic of my heart's new tattoo – "*BigLove*." As a quick introduction to my self-created term "*BigLove*," I offer my definition: it means to walk through something with the intention of an expansive, courageous, and inclusive heart of loving for the situation or person. It means to recognize healthy boundaries and to still hold a heart full of compassion and wisdom to come to whatever is present, with our biggest energy for Being from love. My intention is to actually demonstrate my concept on the pages of this love letter to you.

Element Three – Fierce Forgiveness. This chapter will invite you to a higher, more self-loving consciousness, from which to view all things forgiveness: their deeper meaning, the higher calling, power, and the parts of forgiveness. I will introduce my definition of Queendom. We will explore: how to make the decision to stay or go; what forgiveness is not; the paradox of forgiveness; humility and forgiveness; healing through integration; and why humans cheat. We will learn how to unlearn your old marriage and say "Yes" to the future.

Element Four – Your Super Powers 411. This chapter will invite you to discover your untapped super powers. What they are and how to use them. How they are the path to rebuilding a new love, along with, personal resilience and self-empowerment. We will explore challenges, opportunities and techniques to foster safety for intimacy after betrayal. This is where you learn how to call-in your super powers.

Element Five – Perspective. This chapter will help you see that a shift in perspective is a mighty thing and how to cultivate a practice of looking for the good, the gold, and the silver lining. How to trust your intuition again; and discover an empowering perspective on intention. How to decide what type of detective you will choose to become. How to deal with triggers on the road to healing. How to choose and cultivate your mirror of love. How to own your story, and ultimately how to celebrate you!

Element Six – Radical Self-Care. This chapter will take you through a profound retreat for self-care. This retreat will be a source of nourishment and restorative treatment for your wounded heart and will guide your self-care multi-dimensionally. Starting from the pool of pain you are in now, you will discover ways to begin moving out and through. The heart treatments will include: where to begin to take care of you; revisiting grief; what to do first when you can't face others; and what to do when focus is impossible. How to find someone to talk to: the how, who, when, and where to share. We will also revisit perspective – it's your story to tell; making sense of it all; the world of "whys"; unpacking the "blame/shame game"; how not to kill him; how not to kill yourself; the impermanence of life; and your mirror of love.

Element Seven – Build New Muscles. This chapter will be your call to commitment to daily training using this self-empowering workout; essential to truly move forward. Your workout will cover: the power of empathy/compassion; Ego-lifts: minute-to-minute personal power views. Why forgiveness is a cumulative event; the value of fun; authentic living in front of the kids: how not to pass it on; and how to cultivate comfort with uncertainty. How to engage with your Queenship and other empowering feminine ignitors; and how nothing is wasted: the training opportunities in triggers.

Element Eight – Cultivate Self-Awareness. This chapter will explore the magic of the "hopeful romantic". What it means to "fail forward" with love. How to gently continue to cultivate self-awareness. How to know when you are healing. How to plant the seeds to be inspired, keep faith and have hope. When to take a "heroine's vacay." Finding *BigLove*. More on my view of what it means to be the queen of your Being. Where do we go from here - your heroine's journey!

Dear Precious Beauty,

Are you ready to embark on this daring journey? Well then, with love as our north star, where ever you are, I am with you. Together, let's move forward to the first essential element to healing after betrayal – grief.

Chapter 3:

Grief is Your Source of Grace

"What is to give light must endure burning."
– Viktor E. Frankl

It is my experience that it is not always easy to recognize what is happening in you after this shift in your universe occurs. Under the weighty blanket that has fallen upon your energy, your mind is scrambling to find a safe spot to rest. You wait, frightened, for the big answer to come. But there is only the bad news echoing in your head - yes, it happened. It is real. Still, like a defending attorney representing your heart, you keep coming back to the possibility that there's a good reason, and that it's not your guy's fault. You want to believe he was duped, because there is no way he would do this on his own. How could he? How could this be happening? Being a compassionate investigator, you next move to the possibility that it's somehow your fault. You did or did not do something that ultimately opened the door and caused this mess.

This internal binging of thoughts retriggers a flood of emotional aching bringing in tears and increased waves of sadness and full-on deep despair. It is the permanence and the coming consequences of this event, that lean hard on you. Add to that the acceptance of our mortal impermanence, a genuine recognition that our lives are short, and looking clearly at what a tangled mess there is to deal with now. All this is heightened by the chatter of our egoic mind, advising us as to, what the "logical, reasonable, and responsible you" should do next. Advocating for the anger and the rise-up of madness, and revenge that it hints, may do you service now. It begins to feel therapeutic to shift the audience to other inner voices that bring up a remembrance of the you that was strong, confident, happy, and in-charge of yourself before this betrayal. Your happy confidence that dropped down the trap door when this shift occurred. Now there is only desperate confusion and a wish to wake-up and find it is all just a very bad dream. You struggle to sleep, which only follows your physical and emotional exhaustion from crying. You don't want to wake, because waking only begins the cycle again. You long to see a door that leads out of this new intense emotional cycle you now wholly inhabit.

The reality is surreal, its pain is a profound other dimensional feeling... and for this while, it feels unshakable. It's hard to breathe deeply. It's like your lungs will never expand large enough again to let in a good stream of pure refreshing air. Something is pressing on your Being. It seems hard to imagine it will ever, ever end. Is this the feeling of my new life? Everything is duller and muted and gray.

My precious and courageous friend, frightening as this

feels right now, you are actually alright. What is happening is that you are standing in the currents of grief.

In this chapter, we will explore the first Essential Element – *Grace of Grief*. However, we shall not begin on the topic of grief without first honoring *you*, by acknowledging all that your wisdom has already called you to grieve. Chances are you have already experienced loss, on a number of dimensions, along the journey of your life. Truth is, if we are living and loving, we cannot escape loss or pain. We all have our experiences that have toughened us and made us stronger and brought us new skills to use when loss occurs. You may even believe, as I once did, that you were well prepared to meet whatever challenge your life could dish out, till this bomb flew in from left field and knocked you down.

My intention is to meet you wherever you are and to assure you that you are strong enough, brave enough, brilliant enough, and loving enough to endure "this."

From this space of safety and support, I want to invite you to further consider how grieving betrayal awakens specific aspects of your identity and requires a courageous openness to explore places in you that you may not have considered before.

There is a "love/hate/deny" relationship that many folks have with the unavoidable cycle of life. Everything that lives eventually dies. We all want to say we accept and understand it. You may be like many who believe they know all about grieving. When I have approached the topic of "the need to grieve" with women, the response has been varied. They range from deep curiosity to a drive-by, been-there before avoidance, and everything in between. In review, wounded hearts on the mend deserve non-judgment and a compassionate kindness. What is

worth noting here is that what rises to the surface is an awareness that processing grief requires not just a passing through,
but also the work of transformation to something that feeds your
soul. Then, by integrating this experience into the fabric of your
life, it enables an evolution of your spiritual Being and adds to
your life's quality. We will talk more about this further on.

My experience has shown me that you know best the
grieving that you have experienced, but grief, like living itself,
comes in a variety of energies, colors, or dimensions – whichever description resonates best with you. What I have learned is
that until you've walked in the shoes of the betrayed, you don't
really know how you will get through it. However, what you
are is *prepped* to learn. Everyone lives their experience through
their own life's lens. It is this *uniquely you* lens that defines and
interprets the meaning, the volume, and the feeling of grief for
each of us. We are all beautifully and uniquely different.

I knew a beautiful, loving woman in the elder years of her
wisdom, who had borne many children and lost several of them.
One at childbirth, one at toddler age, another tragically in their
forties. Still, she confided in me that the end of her marriage
was her deepest enduring heartbreak. I read of another beautiful mother whose adult child was mentally ill and refusing
help, and simply roamed the streets, homeless. She wrote with
tremendous despair that she wished her child dead, rather than
bear the unending grief she felt in the knowledge of the daily
suffering her child was going through.

I knew a passionate man whose beloved elderly mother
passed of natural causes while he was in his sixties, and who
mourned for her deeply and daily into his nineties and still
could hardly bear the thought that she had gone.

Another life-survivor, in his elder years, once told me that the end of his second marriage was the worst day of his life. This seemed remarkable given that his beloved first wife had died in their mid-thirties, and his beloved son died later, in his late twenties – both decades before his later marriage ended.

The stories of these lovely people demonstrate what many of us already know – we all experience and respond to traumatic events in our lives, uniquely. We respond based on so many personal factors. It makes sense to consider that each of us will encounter and deal with grief in our own unique way. Our intention on this path together is to stimulate *your freedom* to heal.

My own journey, in search of authentic love, included three divorces. One I left, one left me, and one I was losing my life in. Then, faced with a cancer scare, my desire to live woke-up and I moved out – to divorce.

Each was a loss on some level. Each brought the need to grieve. It wasn't until much later that I realized this. Instead, I just kept bravely moving forward. Without realizing I brought the grief of those experiences forward, sub-consciously and subtly influencing my next living relationship. My belief was that I was in good standing with my past experiences and how I had processed them. I had given them good attention and grieved the aspects that needed to be grieved. Or so I thought. But while on some levels that was true, what I learned when this event of betrayal occurred in my beautiful, safe, and wonderful relationship with my guy, was that there is a lot more to grieving than just crying and reflection and searching for the good.

We know what we know, and we use what we know to support us through the challenges and crisis that rise in living our everyday lives, and in our precious relationships. Until something really digs in deep and imprisons us – holds us hostage and compels us to scout our way out and over the pain – we simply employ the skills, habits, thoughts, and ways of coping that we always did because they have always brought us through. This is beautifully normal. It is human nature to repeat what appears to work and is familiar.

Betrayal digs deep. The wound seems unhealable, and yet we are not ready to give up. We are not ready to let go of all the good we knew. Still, in hindsight, even the good seems suspicious. All the fun and sweet things seem to pose the question: Were those experiences honest? Were they real? What was happening that I should have noticed during those times? Is it my fault this happened because I failed to notice? How can I ever trust him again?

And there is a slice of the heart of the matter. Betrayal is a death of trust.

The pain of a death of trust that I felt with my guy's action of betrayal was like nothing I'd experienced before. I'd been through deaths of family and friends, previous marriages, and I even struggled most of my life feeling betrayed by my mom in a pattern she repeated both with and without mind. All these were profound practices in personal growth. Still, nothing prepared me for the experience of betrayal from the one person I believed with all my heart knew me and loved me like no one before could or would after.

In my grief I felt so duped. I had done so much personal work to grow and evolve into a more open trusting Being; to love more freely and with less judgment; to heal the wounds of my parents and past relationships; to learn how to show up from a place of open kindness and deeper love. My friends recognized a bright warrior-earned resilience in me. With this new wonderful sense of empowerment, I gave to this beautiful man, my guy, and accepted the challenges while giving all the support possible to our world and our love. Then one day – *bam!* And in that moment the trust I had in him died. The place of comfort, safety and protection disappeared. All the parts of me that felt whole with him – felt shattered.

The event of betrayal is an event of emotional death. It's an end to something that was real and alive. A living protective cocoon for your treasured marital identity. In my own event, my gift of intimacy given felt tossed, disrespected, and then replaced by embarrassment, vulnerability, victimization, and a sense of complete loss. A loss of safety, love, laughter, focus, everything that defined my love and relationship.

Intimate closeness suddenly feels foreign and removed. There's a sense of loss of intimate ownership, when you felt he was yours and you were his. All these foundations of belief now are cracked or crumbled. These are a few of the effects of an emotional death by betrayal.

Both death of trust and death of an emotion lead to a point most important to you, my wounded friend, which is these conditions form a death of the marriage as you knew it. This is hard to hear I agree, but breathe deeply, beauty, and read on. There is good news in this which we will explore together soon.

The pain and grief from betrayal is hard to bear. It is not better, worse, or equal to anything else. It is genuine, profound, painful grief just as it comes up in you. It is your unique experience. The relevance of this point is to bring attention to the cultural practice of comparing. Folks may say, "well, it's not as bad as when the airplane fell from the sky." What I advocate is to let yourself remain free of comparisons and self-judgment. A powerful question you can ask yourself, to engage each element on this path to healing, and especially when processing your grief is: *What am I willing to feel?* Opening to whatever that willingness invites, will take all the courage and strength you've got, so remember, you are more powerful than you know.

All things are connected in life. I don't know if you are open to the concept of energy and the connectedness of all things. I hope with this experience, you will see the value in being open to it because it holds power that you can call upon. Grief itself is powerful. I invite you to recognize the powerful gifts that appear.

One of the gifts of higher power and soul-beauty for you, from grief – is called Grace. Grace is the willingness and ability to forgive. It is a spiritual touch that comes with your invitation and ignites an awareness of the profound connectedness of every other level of energy along the path from grief to forgiveness and beyond. Grace appears as your softened heart ignites compassion, widening your view to believe forgiveness is possible. Grief is the source of your experience with Grace because it is grief that gives way to the opportunity to soften your heart. A heart unknowingly hardened for protection throughout our lives so that we can survive in the land of the things that scare us. Interwoven in these pages, it is my intention to illuminate the opportunities to invite and embrace Grace into your experience as it appears.

Now more good news. The recognition that betrayal is a death does not mean that there is no hope. You can reinvent and revive a new stronger version of your marriage. It is possible. I did it and so can *you*. There is a lot that must be aligned and agreed upon between you and your love, before the decision is set, and further in, we will break it down, I promise. So stay with me and we will look at the basic stages of grief and what you can do in each of them to plant seeds of beauty in this breakdown.

With the remaining part of this chapter, my intention is to invite you to focus in on your experience of grief from betrayal as we get very specific about how you can choose to move through your grief in a way that lovingly serves you. To open up to transformational ways you can move through your grief into a self-empowering openness to begin healing and to generate the dedicated energy you will need so that you can engage yourself, your life, and most importantly your marriage.

Grief is a natural human energy. You are most likely familiar with it as an emotion. The term "emotion" means energy in motion. So let's review the basic stages recognized in the emotion of grief, and along the way I will share what I have learned on this path that is self-empowering and profoundly self-loving.

As you feel a resistance to accept that this element is necessary, keep in mind this point: If you truly live, then loss and grief are unavoidable. And, grief comes whether you acknowledge it or not. What is of extraordinary and life-changing value to you comes from what you choose to do with it. It's worth repeating over and over.

It may have happened this morning, yesterday, last week, last month or years ago – if this book is resonating with you, then chances are you have wounds that need to be tended to. I want to honor where you are coming from: you might be in shock, still in denial, in the twist of anger and rage, or falling deeply into the overwhelming pit of despair over your broken heart. You may even believe you are over it. However, if there remains something about it that unexpectedly still sticks in your throat, jabs pins in your heart, or causes an uprising of anger that feels like bugs chewing at your soul, then welcome, friend. Grief is the place to begin.

Allow me a little background perspective about the stages we will cover. There is much written about grief, the stages and so forth. Some professionals who have studied grief say there are seven stages, others say five stages. Guided by my experience, allow me to round them out and explore them as:

1. shock/denial
2. pain/heartbreak
3. anger/rage
4. depression/reflection
5. acceptance/choice

These stages will be explored one at a time. However, your personal experience of stages can occur in any order and in any combination. The value is in your awareness, your engagement of the opportunities and the forward self-compassionate thoughts and actions you choose within.

Now that we've tilled the soil, let's plant some seeds of awareness.

Stage One – Shock/Denial

The first second after the event occurs, we are already in Stage One. Our response of shock or denial is our human system's protective response to physical, mental or emotional trauma. We are stunned into a state of disbelief, which then slows everything down to give us space, to attempt to make sense of what just happened.

How we present in our state of shock varies. Hard silence, screaming, collapse, seclusion, escape, lashing out, rationalization, hostile confrontation, and so on … any of these are possible. Denial shows up as our minds struggle not to believe the facts we have been presented. There must be another explanation. This simply cannot be true. Period. Power is exerted on the believability of the story. So, if you don't believe the story, it didn't happen. How could it? The only acceptable explanation is anything else but the truth.

In some ways in this first stage, there is a small amount of hopeful power that is being employed. After all, your mind clings to alternate possibility so that there is hope. The time spent in this stage is whatever your world allows. If you are isolated, have no family or friends and few obligations, you may hang here awhile. However, if you are a woman who chooses each day to live authentically, engaged and connected to friends, family and community … this will not be a long stay.

Whatever your circumstance, here are a couple of helpful steps (note: recognize that this work is big work – keep in mind, this book only offers steps to begin) for moving forward:

Be gentle with yourself. Recognize that you are an injured heart. A death has occurred. You have lost something precious to you. You will need a little time to acclimate for an opening to the truth. You will require some big time TLC. Whatever that means to you – make that your mission to define and fill for yourself. One requirement: be sure it is healthy for your body and your soul. Learn to breath, meditate, walk, journal, rest, and be quiet with yourself. Remember to hydrate, to nourish your body and your thoughts.

Whatever you choose to initially do in response to your partner's act of betrayal, choose wisely. Or don't choose action at all. Not until you can feel your toes again. Though actions and words can generally be righteously defended from this stage of grief, remembering that they can still leave a lasting mark in the universe, is meaningful to your well-being. When we hold to that higher truth, as best we can, we give back to ourselves from self-compassion. More love is possible from this place. And from this place you can open to stage two.

Stage Two – Pain/Heartbreak

Once shock and denial thin out and the facts you know glare brightly in your eyes, there is no holding back the flow of tears and pain from your broken heart. This pain has no outer limit. It is as boundless as you will allow yourself to feel.

There are times when I felt as though the pain was too much to bear. I would call upon anything that reminded me of my own strength to bear more. To feel it all. To open the flood gates and allow the pain to be felt. I would think of the line in the movie *Out of Africa* where Karen explains how she trains to bear her pain of loneliness by letting herself feel it and when she thinks she can't bear anymore – she challenges herself to stay open and bear it for one more minute. This left her feeling she could bear anything. I use that trick as one way, among many, to practice in staying open to the pain. I believed if I let myself feel and be in it – it would pass through me and I could move on. I soon found out that it could feel never ending like the constant ocean tides. It required a brave faith in myself to bear it and a faith that nothing lasts forever. That even this would pass. During this time, the only place I seemed to find rest came from sleep due to emotional exhaustion.

This stage of grief is the place where your broken-open heart gets fired in the oven on its way to rising to potential for reshaping and rebirth. The agony of this heartache wears the hard walls down to begin the softening of your energy. It's a bit like the over exertion of muscles when you just can't lift one more thing. The tank is empty. The space is clear. It is in the open clearing that you can wait for something new and ready to sprout. A mindfulness must be given to what "that" is to be. Pain can push you to the darkness or to the light. You have choice.

During this stage in the fire you weep from awareness of your vulnerability, your feelings of shame that this happened in your relationship; and of blame that perhaps, in some way you caused it. You weep as you feel pain from the meaning you give this act of betrayal. The meaning you choose to apply to yourself. Interpreting it to undeniably mean that you are undeserving, misunderstood, unappreciated, without value, invisible and unlovable. In this state of break down, you feel that something has come apart that can never be put back together again. It is all about the flow of pain from the open channel coming from your heartbreak. This stage can be present intensely for weeks or months. Everyone is unique.

Seeking Professional Help

Depression is normal in this stage. In grief, there is a sense of depression. It can feel like deep depression and still be in the range of moving through grief. Moving through still holds the awareness that you are in the pit of pain but that there is going to be a light at the end of the tunnel, at some point, some day. There is hope.

When you start to feel hopeless, an awareness of the depth, length, intensity of your depression is important. It is crucial to be aware of when you may need professional help, that is when it is shifting into clinical depression. You still have everyday life, you must move forward within. Therefore, if depression is intensely persistent for more time than you can comfortably allow, or you begin to descend into feelings of hopelessness, and it prevents you from working or leaving your home, or if unending crying takes on the feeling of being completely out of control, seek help for all these mentioned chronic conditions. Be kind to yourself and find a way to seek professional medical help. It is not uncommon that your processing of grief might require some extra help and medical support, so that you can rest, be calmed, and then reengage in moving forward for health. My friend, seeking medical help when the need is indicated is courageous self-love at work, so please embrace it.

Practices to Comfort and Support

In Stage Two, after you have been processing heartache and pain for a while, and begin to feel yourself moving forward, there is an awareness that the waves of grief begin coming less frequently but are still present on your path. This heartache takes as long as it takes. Let yourself feel what comes. It is like the rain, cleaning the sky, tears express the pain and allow it to move through you. This is the path to healing. As the intensity eases a bit, and you begin to simply feel the softer levels of sadness of the heartbreak and grief, you will seek comfort in many ways. I offer a few suggestions to support the comfort you seek.

ca Open to whatever practices bring you a sense of release. Allow yourself tears, listen to music, journal, rearrange the house, clean, cook, paint, meditate, pray, sleep, read – look for the "thing" or activity that brings you the energy to express whatever you are feeling. I remember going to hot yoga and feeling completely relaxed as my tears went unnoticed within the humid, perspiration provoked, class. Then ending in corpse pose, relaxed, spent and open to receive the final openhearted blessing seemed to bring deeper release and comfort. Like feeling safe, while in pain, out in the open. Invite yourself to *feel* in this stage. To find places that comfort, and practices that support you.

ca One great practice to explore and engage is Tonglen Meditation. I found it most empowering as guided by Pema Chodron. I encourage you check it out. There is something profoundly powerful when you engage in this intention to stay with your feelings, and while you do, to offer compassionate energy with intention, for the easing of other's suffering, while you are suffering. It is a powerful tool when you find it hard to manage difficult feelings or responses. I have used it in many difficult times with spirit enriching and self-empowering results.

ca Envision your strong self on vacation, while your heart-broken self is working hard at this self-loving emoting practice. This concept allows you to own your strength while opening to your softer self with the suffering you are working through.

ଓ Another practice that I found helpful was to give in to my sense of need to move all the pictures of my guy and I from my view. Regardless of whether I was sad or angry when I did. I felt it gave me a choice to start over and create a new view, a new story, of our old pictures when the time was right. This was very cathartic for me and reduced the triggering of pain I would suddenly feel as I saw the pictures of our lovely times past. Over time, I'd put them up and take them down as my heart began to heal. Today they are all appreciated again. Do this with whatever feels self-compassionate to you. Give yourself gentle space for this important work.

ଓ Take your time with your broken heart. It will take time to mend. Believe it will mend and make a powerful choice to keep believing it even when it doesn't feel like it. Choose to believe or imagine something greater than you can feel right now; that it is waiting there for you to open to it. Explore the notion of the power of the largest love that reaches around the globe. See yourself in a powerful love-field of energy – because you are. Engage in readings or movies that validate the pain you are feeling, to help you remember, that you are not alone. Love and pain are connected to each other. Even if love starts where pain leaves off, you can't have one without the risk of the other. You can't truly live without love or pain. Do research that fuels a mind and spirit journey to support you, and to validate the value of exactly where you are. This validation will feed you strength for living forward.

ୠ Try this: Allow yourself to imagine you are sitting comfortably in a loving-energy field. Feet planted on the floor. Palms facing the sky, relax them, in each other, on your lap. Close your eyes. Feel and breathe deeply into your body's energy. Feel the subtle vibration of your living body. Imagine it vibrating out to the edges of your space. Fill the space with your color of love. Feel yourself floating in it. Imagine your healing heart being held in a cradle of loving-kindness. Feel the love there for you. Breathe and relax in it. Practice as needed.

Once your spirit has endured the fire and your heart has begun to soften, you begin to feel vulnerable again. That's when an organic inner search begins for what you believe will be a smarter, protective, and stronger emotion – which sparks in our wounded heart as anger/rage.

Stage Three – Anger/Rage

During the previous Stage Two, allowing in the feelings of your heartbreak, the strongest sense of yourself that you name, generally feels like weakness, vulnerability and helplessness to the pain coming up in you. Your natural self-preservation instincts motivate you to seek aid in places that bring strong energy. Enter Stage Three – Anger/Rage. You become angry when you feel the violation of your happiness and peace of mind that has occurred at the hands of your trusted love. It is in this stage that the "How dare you! How could you!" and all the other vitriol arrows you feel the righteous freedom to shoot – fire from your powerful pain-driven energy. You are filled with the indignant energy of feeling right. That you are right, and he is wrong. You are so right that your angry energy feeds righteous permission to whatever's cooking in your protectively engaged reptilian mind. This roll of thunder erupts inside and feeds the view that it's time to get the big battle cry out and aired, rather than crying your eyes out, in bed. There is no doubt in your mind that you were wronged. Exerting your power may begin with a low controlled tone, as you deliberately wade into the issue at hand, demanding the why, the where, the how, and the when ... of it all. However, in your weakened state it can escalate to loud bursting accusations and protests, which move to all out cursing the source of your broken heart. You can become narrowly focused on letting him know without any question, about the suffering he has caused. Then become determined to give him a pay-back for the suffering he has brought down upon your heads. Rage can develop from the onset, or rise as the engagement to discuss begins to go sideways.

In this stage, everything feels like it should be discussed, dissected, and explained until you are in less pain. The truth is – nothing should be discussed in this stage. Your brain is not capable of coming from the places that will serve you. You can only come from a place of survival and that provokes your reptilian brain to engage. It says, *"Eat him before he eats you."* While this may be a momentarily good visual, if your goal is to truly heal in your marriage – you most likely will hinder your success if you eat him first.

In the stage of anger/rage, there is a desperate mind-search in progress to make sense out of all this and an angry investigation only brings you more pain as you unravel and find more evidence of the wrong-doings that you already know happened. Digging yourself deeper and deeper into pain. Your level-headed dependable reasoning, which used to serve you so well, produces the opposite effect now. Soon you realize that the more you try to make sense out of this nonsense, or, try to find an answer that you can live with, the more you realize you can't. You come to see it's real, it happened, and you can't undo that. You can't change this fact no matter how brilliant, beautiful or strong you are. This reality grinds down deeper as you continue your frustrating search, and only serves to make you madder about the emerging inevitability and perceived permanence of the pain that your guy has brought home to your marriage.

You have every right to feel the anger and violation that you feel. Let yourself feel it. Don't suppress or deny it. However, choose very mindfully, how, when, where and with whom you express it. Anger is an emotion that also must be allowed to move through you. Still it is critical for your intention to heal that you appreciate that once your anger is spent, you will still need to live in the "house" (your Being) it came from, so mindful anger is essential. This is a very hard training but doable. You are wounded, dear friend, and although anger feels stronger – it actually comes from feeling a loss of control and safety in your marriage. It comes from your new perspective of feeling like you are a victim. That you have been violated on an energetic and emotional level. Your heart has been broken, wounded – and you have experienced an emotional trauma. If you want to heal, your strength to heal will come from noticing how you are naming your situation and then making a decision to shift. The healing you seek will come from shifting your view about *yourself* in what has occurred. Choose the view that you are not a victim. That who you are is a beautiful, strong enough, brave enough, powerfully loving-large enough woman, capable of feeling your anger for the hurt, but with immense capacity to hold compassion in the other hand for the human imperfections we all possess. Choose to see your guy in his vulnerability. Human and perfectly imperfect as we all are. Choose how you will voice your intense disappointment and anger. And let it be tempered with your most genuine message of intention to heal and positively revive the injured parts of your marriage, yourself and your love for your guy. Demand time and require mutual effort to kindness, as the pieces try to come back together in a new lovingly authentic and rededicated relationship. Ask for gentle space to allow the anger to move organically and find ways to practice with the anger. Hold intention to bringing you closer to knowing yourself, your strength, your beauty - all with self-love and acceptance.

Here are a few powerful ways to train: Meditate, practice mindfulness with how you feel, speak, think, act then journal on it. See and hear yourself without judgment. Journal about how you want to show up each day and meditate with the intention. Choose to come from a loving energy each day. Practice speaking in a lower tone. Exercise to sweat for energetic release. Read about the emotion of anger. Journal about all the anger that rises in you and express it as freely in writing as you wish. You can always toss or destroy it after. Or keep it and find ways to shift your energy. Acknowledge your feelings and know they are OK when you are writing them. Honor the purpose in the practice.

About revenge. In this stage of anger and/or rage it is normal for the thought of getting even to rise. An "eye for an eye" sounds fair when your heart has been broken. The illusion of satisfaction from seeking revenge seems comforting from your wounded place, as are the images of revenge gone wild, mentally flashing visuals of: crashed cars, torched houses, nasty phone calls, social media exposure and rants, ripped clothes, broken pictures, tossed belongings, burned, buried, and just generally destroyed things associated with the other. Your world feels destroyed so it's your turn to destroy. In truth revenge serves no one. It doesn't turn back time and it doesn't improve the future. It only adds to the painful baggage of the present. Your power is your choice of how you show up in the experience. Choose well, sweet heart. Revenge brings a long-lasting negative chain reaction that is like dumping trash in the ocean. It floats out riding the current to spread destruction and harm to lives long after the memory of the trash you tossed has passed. Choose to care about your response. It's hard, so hard from this deeply wounded place but it's not impossible. Choose the counsel of gentle friends who will love and support you in avoiding a destructive response. Watch movies that demonstrate the worst-case outcomes of those who chose to seek revenge. Live each day with love and healing as your focus.

As you notice your anger has eased, allowing in a more grounded feeling of compassion you will move into Stage Four – Depression/Reflection.

Stage Four – Depression/Reflection

By this stage, there is a residing sadness that seems stuck to you. It's gentler than the full-on agony you once felt, but the presence of it keeps happiness at bay. You can feel it. You feel softer, worn out and down. Your pep is off. You are pushing through the days but there is a film of sadness. Your energy still feels a little flat. You notice it and you look for relief. This is the beginning of the upturn. It might not sound like it, but it is. In this subtle depressed state, your heart is kneaded soft and ready to be reformed. The home of your heart has experienced a massive windstorm and the debris has been blown through. Grief allows the release of the painful energy produced by the event. Without grief all the pain, shame, blame, anger, rage, depression would just sit trapped in your heart and body. If you decide you can't or won't stay with the grief; to practice moving through these stages of emotions toward healing – then you're headed in the direction of the land of bitterness. Bitterness takes residence in your heart when you embrace the fear of feeling your feelings, or refuse to release the anger, and instead allow stubborn, angry, defensive, righteousness to become the boss of your Being. Unfortunately, the longer you let bitterness sit in you, the bigger and stronger bitterness grows, because it eats everything good that comes to you and transforms it into more of what bitterness already is, disappointment and resentment.

Depression slows you down. You can't do things quickly when you feel sad. The slowing down allows a precious gap to appear so that the light of hope and compassion can begin to peek out again from your heart. All the practicing and med-itation begins to quiet the monkey mind that came to town (in your thoughts) with this event. It makes way for you to notice, rest, build, practice, feel, think, appreciate, and choose. It opens your whole energy gently to reflection on the possibility that what you want – is possible. In this first part of the stage, this depression is more about softening and slowing into this gentle sadness. You are still gracefully mourning; accept that in you. My experience has shown me that simply acknowledging what you feel in this stage is powerful. When I felt under the weather,

I would take on only the things I could. I would pass on invitations if I didn't feel up to it. I would allow myself to own that I felt depressed or sad, and that was OK. It would pass. All emotions do, but for now, I was choosing self-love and care.

Self-acceptance and self-compassion were the topics I chose to fill my soul with. I would journal the questions I had, then mindfully notice what would come up in answer to them. What do these answers really mean to me? How do I practice them? These paths led to more reflections on what self-love means. How do you engage to build these systems in yourself? We will explore these further on. For now, it is only important that you realize and celebrate that you are in the fertile space of opening to greater healing and love.

Here are a few things to practice with:
- ∞ Notice what you are feeling.
- ∞ Journal all around what comes up in you.
- ∞ Meditate.
- ∞ Lots of self-care.
- ∞ Be gentle with yourself.
- ∞ Fill your soul with inspirational and loving content.
- ∞ Do things that feel good and practice reflecting on a loving vision for your marriage.
- ∞ Practice all the things that have felt helpful or comforting from the previous suggestions offered.

You are evolving.

Sometimes this can sound all "pie in the sky". Things suddenly feel better. Then they feel worse. But stay mindful of the truth which is this is hard work. There is a concept known as – "wash, rinse and repeat" – in life coach training. Simply put, you try something new, you fall down, then you get up, and start over. In this healing process there is a lot to work through and it takes as much time as it takes.

As reflection, and practices invite a new expansiveness of thought, you begin to feel a strength you didn't realize was there for you and this is the beginning of Stage Five: Acceptance/Choice.

Stage Five – Acceptance/Choice

This is the launching pad from which healing begins to feel real. You have mourned, emoted, felt everything and practiced for the sake of opening to more expansive love. You have warrior-ed through, and what is here for you now is treasure for your soul. You have endured the burning and are ready for the light to emerge. Here is where you have the strength to bravely look at your marriage and recognize that it is dead. The marriage you knew before has died. You can look without blame, shame, or the need to place guilt anywhere. You understand now that accepting the death of your old marriage opens to some good news. The hard reality is your previous marriage was already broken. Now that you have honored it with your path through grief, you are ready to make clear decisions about what to do next. You have accepted that betrayal has occurred. You have accepted that all Beings are perfectly imperfect, and your guy is no different. You have grown in the understanding that being betrayed is not an act that defines your worth or who you are. What you do in response to it is what matters. You have committed to one of the most challenging and courageous acts of compassion and love – forgiveness.

It is in the effort of forgiveness that both you, your guy and your marriage can find healing. Your marriage will never be the same. That's the good news. Embrace it and see the blank canvas in front of you. What do you want your marriage to look like? Who do you need your husband to become in your new marriage? Who do you need to become in your new marriage? What are the needs, expectations, and wants of your marriage? How will you both choose to communicate them? How will you both deal with the parts that are still tricky? What can you do when it gets hard? Because it will. For a while, it will. Where should you begin?

You could begin where I did – opening the cage my fear put us in. During the anger stage, I recall noticing that no matter how hard I tried I couldn't seem to stay away from my anger. After much reflection, practice, coaching and hard work – I realized that I had put my guy and I in a cage and tossed the key away from us. There we flew around and round looking for an escape from our struggle with each other. Not realizing our pattern, we simply continued to repeat it. We would exhaust ourselves with our attempts to connect which escalated from first trying not to be angry, but only wanting to talk it out, which lead to arguing, then to crying, then to apologizing, and then wanting to start over. I kept at it to prove I was committed to forgiving. That cage contained pain. Pain that I believed I had worked through. Still, I seemed to keep resurrecting it.

Until one day I made the mindful choice to stop requiring him to be worthy of my forgiveness, as a requirement of engaging him from my energy of kindness and forgiveness. I wasn't aware that this is what I was doing until it revealed itself to me. My practice of mindfulness paid off. I made the choice to be responsible for my happiness. I made the choice to open the cage and release both of us. I gave myself the courageous permission to treat him as though I had already forgiven him. This is harder than it sounds, but it is key to this healing.

This was the light that appeared in the distance as I continued toward the end of the tunnel of grief. My friend, grief is a process. There is no way to predict or plan how it will move for you. Just when you think it is over, something arises that unexpectedly triggers something that pulls you back into that space a bit or a lot. Don't let this discourage you. See whatever arises as *for you*. There is simply more healing needed; that is all it is indicating. Be patient and self-compassionate. Notice where you are feeling hooked, notice what feeling is there, and what it is saying to you. Notice where you might need to more deeply explore the meaning of the hooks still there. With kindness and acceptance of wherever you are, recommit to intentionally softening, choose to reignite your healing without self-judgment or judgment of your husband, and choose to embrace the healing of love.

Now that we have moved through my final stage of grief and explored acceptance and choice – it is time to step forward on this path to Essential Element Two – Your Essence of Love.

Chapter 4:

Your Essence of Love – *"BigLove"*

"It is not inertia alone that is responsible for human relationships repeating themselves from case to case, indescribably monotonous and unrenewed: it is shyness before any sort of new, unforeseeable experience with which one does not think oneself able to cope. But only someone who is ready for everything, who excludes nothing, not even the most enigmatical will live the relation to another as something alive."
– Rainer M. Rilke

L ovely friend, you would think that writing a chapter on love would be easy. Love is an essential part of everything human. We all know this. Right? Of course. However, do you know its purpose or power? Have you ever really wondered about it? Or about where it really comes from?

There are plenty of books on the topic of love and the how to of it all. How to attract it, find it, keep it, what to do after you lose it... etc. They're all out there already for you to explore. So, in writing this letter of love to you, I asked myself – what do I want to share with you about love? What did I want or need to know about love when I was searching for the "thing" that would lead me to open to mending my broken heart and would support my intention to heal and forgive my guy? Further, what curiosity do I want to invite in you by the end of the chapter?

I remembered that when I was where you are, I wanted to begin to understand what love meant to *me*. I asked myself, "What do I really know about love? What does self-love, self-acceptance, self-worth really mean? What are boundaries?" I had heard about coming from love and being love, and I truly thought I was evolving on that path until my event … so then I wondered, did I really know? I realized my answer was there. If I was asking the questions, I must have had a need for more answers. So, let's explore in this chapter, Essential Element Number Two Your Essence of Love – *BigLove*. I want to share what I learned and what supported my healing. My invitation to you is to let this chapter inspire your curiosity for your beautiful resident power.

Seeking Love

I can still visualize my guy coming down the outdoor hall in high school – walking toward me. The late afternoon sun softening in a background glow. His gait, his football jacket, his widening smile, and the exhilarated emotions that my young hidden love felt at the very sight of him. Images and feelings that stayed locked in my memory for forty years and remain as vivid today. What is remarkable is that we didn't have a lot of time together, back then. We had one extraordinary date and a few brief times we were able to spend some time in each other's company. Beyond that, we were limited by our shyness and captivity of our perceived separate future paths. So, for forty years, as we moved forward in our lives, we were just memories to each other. I had no intention or belief we would be together again. Treasured sweet romantic memories stored away, risen and manifested as we showed-up in each other's world again, out of the blue, while on opposite sides of the world.

In those years of separate lives, I was married and divorced three times. I knew nothing about romance, love, relationship, or intimacy in my youth. My upbringing (with all love and due respect to my dear deceased parents), realistically only prepared me for a long-term gig in a nunnery. My folks neither spoke of nor modeled healthy intimacy. Entering young relationship terrain, I only had two guidelines with which to navigate. They were: the unspoken things I shouldn't do and the unspoken things absolutely forbidden to do. I was a fully militant virgin in body and mind, afraid of any act named "sin" – as I entered my first marriage at twenty-two. I birthed two children and opted-out before my thirtieth birthday, when I realized I didn't *feel* loved.

My next two marriages were entered: one, out of fear of being alone, and my last from fear of losing the man I believed I could enjoy enduring love with for the rest of my life. None of these marriages brought me real happiness. And *there* is where, I discovered my problem. I believed that marriage would "bring" or "make" me happy. I didn't know my destiny was to find happiness and love on my own, in myself. I was looking for a mirror in someone else that would hold a reflection of me that I could love. A reflection that would show me my value, my worth, my lovability, my happiness. I was operating from a place of deep need. Plus my limiting belief about the importance of the perceptions of others, in my third marriage, concretized my commitment to stay for life, no matter what. I believed anything short of that would reinforce my sense of shame, deeply implanted by my catholic education and upbringing.

As my third marriage deteriorated, my sadness deepened along with my shame. That is, until divine intervention woke me up and this awakening allowed my own brilliance to lead me out. I had been searching for answers even during my decline. Even in the midst of the end of that life experience, I believed that I had learned more about myself and found a new wisdom to move forward with.

Enter my new guy. I believed I had found my "mirror" of lovability, with this beautiful new man of my "literal" dreams. I believed I had invested all the love I had to give in such a way that I was shielded from any hurt, pain, and especially betrayal because it just couldn't happen. Well, how wrong can one be? Very wrong.

Yet, what I found trigged by my guy's event of betrayal and my subsequent desire to heal and forgive was a fire-spark for a new and deeper search for answers within myself. So, I started with the big question: what does happiness or love really, really mean to me?

Our reconnection began, as I said, out of the blue. We spent most of our time apart. As we wrote emails of correspondence back and forth, we each fell deeper in love with each other. We communicated often and in as many ways as possible for years.

Up until the event, I believed we had created a strong love and connection that would protect me from pain. Post-event, I began to wonder if I hadn't actually fallen in love with the *me* that I had become in sending him love letters. Especially when I later realized that my "definition" of "love letter" wasn't what had consistently come back. This curiosity sparked my search for – Who am I? What does love mean to me? Do I know what I want from love? Can this beautiful man, I created in my heart, now manifested, fulfill my needs and wants, even *after* he's now broken my heart?

What is your romantic story of the beginning of your love with your guy? Do you remember the look, the phrase, the moment where your heart was taken captive by his Being? Give this a good ponder. Connecting to the energy of this memory and space of love in you will bring your most powerful energy of love, compassion, soft heart, and openness. These qualities are needed to begin to look at all the whys you are weighing, in order, to stay and heal your marriage, and your heart. I invite you to pause – allow yourself to mentally visit and then journal the moment when your romantic energy woke-up to his. It is your story and it is your key of love to turn in the ignition of healing. Journal it and then let's move on to explore ways to marinate the questions that rise in you around this large unlimited concept of love.

As I researched for answers there were so many books that opened me up to larger and larger views of love. Views on what is the meaning of life itself? Although I was born an empathetic Being, early on, I had to learn to close much of the world out, to protect myself. As I slowly evolved with each thread of new hard-earned wisdom, I learned to pay attention to everything with a new more courageous curiosity. Even the deaths of my beloved, and yes, difficult parents. The death of my guy's beloved mom and dad. The deaths of my sweet little yorkies. I found myself dedicated to providing a loving journey for each of them to have a graceful dignified death. What I experienced was a surreal opening to a field of energy and love I hadn't known before. Exquisite love that even with the tapping out of these letters brings a vibration to my Being. My point, my lovely friend is to invite you to view this path of healing with an expansive lens and see what comes for you.

Let's begin to explore the big questions: Who are You? What is Your Essence of Love?

Who Are You?

This is the existential question of the ages. Right? It is the million, billion, big dollar question. What my experience has shown me is, it is the curious asking about that question, which is the big and juicy part of it. The quest is to know ourselves deeply. Holy-cow. Do you know how many people don't want to know? They don't want to know who they truly are. There is a fear that who they are, may be someone they won't like, and then what will they do? Herein lies the rub. In order to know ourselves, we must journey into that scary territory with the willingness to believe that whatever we find, we will have the ultimate power to handle it, while understanding that we can change whatever we don't like. You can become the Being you are meant to be. You can believe in yourself, even before anyone else does. My experience has shown me that it is easier if someone else believes in you first, because they shine a light of confidence on your deeper capacity, giving you permission to believe in yourself. So, my friend, allow me. I have a deep confidence and belief in you. You have a brilliant light within and you can shine it.

At one point, early on in my search for deeper inner exploration, one of my wonderful friends recommended *The untethered soul* by Michael A. Singer. I made a note, filed it away, and forgot about it. I had lots of other books I was diving into with a ferocious energy and commitment to understand myself. When my event occurred, I fortuitously came across the note and felt a pull to take a look at his book. What I found in his book was that Mr. Singer spoke of who we are in a profoundly enlightening way, and he offered powerful perspectives in my quest to find the answers I was looking for.

First and foremost, his message confirmed my acceptance that we are energy. That there is a more profound reality to our existence in our Being, more than we can humanly hold in thought each minute of every day. This is truly mind-blowing. Next, while to try to exist in that realm too firmly, pulls us sideways from our ability to engage in doing the everyday things we must, we can still practice mindfully exploring within. We can hold intention to evolve, this is both powerful and possible. And finally, that *it is* within our power to engage and employ – but it does require a soul level of commitment.

You are energy. Envision the notion of yourself as energy with the forms you are familiar with: Chakras, Chi, Shakti, Spirit, Consciousness, Soul, or "The Field" (a term coined by author Lynne McTaggart). All these concepts (and there are many more) are defined as life force, energy force or collective consciousness energy fields, within your Being and in relationship to the connectedness of all living things. Each of these concepts offers a window into the deeper questions of: "Who am I and What am I?" Big questions; worthy of exploration.

Exploring these concepts adds to your layers of understanding the vastly profound questions regarding your existence. You notice with deeper curiosity the voices in your head. The thoughts that you believe and those you wish would stop. You actively participate in the wrestling between your felt currents of confidence and your monkey mind's wounded ego. You accept that you are the witness inside of yourself who hears and sees yourself. When you become aware of these and other portholes to your inner knowing, you access a self-empowerment to engage in your life differently. You can begin to wake up to your own life.

Why is this important to this love letter on healing and forgiving? Because we are talking about pain and your desire to heal as you move through it to love. Understanding the purpose of pain and the natural consistent knee-jerk reaction to move away from it at all costs, is essential to opening-up yourself for pure and deep love. You cannot live your life afraid to love in order to avoid pain and hurt. To experience love you must be vulnerable and practice keeping your heart open. It is the closing of your heart that builds the protective wall which block all the healing you desire. Healing which is necessary to rebuild your marriage.

You are light and energy. Each painful experience wounds you, and in turn that experience applies a protective layer on you, like a scab on a wound, layer after layer until your light cannot shine through. You are meant to be a Being of love; empowered with your energy force of *BigLove*, self-love, expansive love. You are challenged to stay open and courageous to accept and experience what comes into your life. You have a body, ignited by the miraculous energy source within you. *All this is to say, this event, your event of being betrayed, can either be seen as, the ruin of your life, or a spark to explore who you truly are.* The *Who Am I* journey is a beginning to a beautiful experience. It is a journey of love to yourself. So, let's continue into more love.

As Rainer Maria Rilke says, "Believe in a love that is being stored up for you like an inheritance, and have faith that in this love there is a strength and a blessing so large that you can travel as far as you wish without having to step outside it." Your inheritance of love is waiting for you to claim it. What more perfect time than now to tap into this wealth of love inside you.

What is your essence of love? What is the essence of anything? The Google Dictionary defines it as "the intrinsic nature or indispensable quality of something, especially something abstract, that determines its character. A property or group of properties of something without which it would not exist or be what it is. Synonyms include: quintessence, soul, spirit, heart, core, nucleus, nitty-gritty…"

Authors Drs. Jette Psaris and Marlena S. Lyons, explain in their powerfully inspiring book, *Undefended Love* – that our essence "is our innate defining substance. It is not the person we have learned to be or have been conditioned to believe we are, not our personality, but the most authentic part of us, in the most distilled form. It is elemental." What my experience has brought to light for me is that we have a core energy of love that we were born with. It is the magnificent bright star at the core of who we are, if all else was removed. It is the shining spirit of ourselves. In the movies, *The Abyss* and *Cocoon*, both gave their best visual sense of the "soul," "love-energy," or "essence" of the alien Beings, but I see them as an inviting visual depiction of our essence. Our radiant energy, which is love at our deepest most essential center. Drs. Psaris and Lyons offer their inspiring insight into these two concepts of "essential Self" and "essential nature." Our essential nature, they explain, can also be referred to as our True Nature, our Original Face, and other names. It is never changing, impersonal and formless. Then there is our essential Self. This, they describe as our uniqueness. To further clarify, they ask us to imagine a beautiful, clear night sky filled with bright, shining stars. "Now imagine the stars as cut-aways, letting light beyond pass through them. That all-pervasive light from beyond is our essential nature, and the light that takes on the shape and form of each star is our essential Self. We all share the same essential nature, that all-pervasive light, but each of us is a separate and unique manifestation of it."

Imagine the freedom and joy of a happy baby whose eyes engage in your gaze and with no effort at all send waves of buoyant love and lightness beaming into your Being with their giggle, and sparkle of wonder. With a complete sense of freedom to be just who they truly are – the physical manifestation of absolute love. Especially since they have not had the exposure to learn who the world around them thinks they need to be, to be loved. Without effort the baby's essence glows out from within. The baby's essence is radiant *love*.

You grew up in the environment you were born into and as you encountered the bumps and scrapes of growing-up, your light was gradually covered over, layer by layer, in the name of defense, protection, and fear. What if you were to begin to entertain the notion that you are a powerful Being of Love? What if, you could envision yourself as a love goddess, a queen, a spirit … or a resilient warrior woman? Choose whichever feminine, self-empowering, grounding image connects and resonates with you. It is the willingness to see yourself as a powerfully loving Being that holds the invitation here.

But wait, my powerfully evolving friend, this invitation is not a path of easy travel. No, it is not. To journey this path to your radiant light of love, it requires courage to face the places in you that need healing. Healing of your own deep wounds formed in the making of *you*. The *you* you have become in your life. Layer upon layer, unhealed wounds block your full essence of love-light, which is your birthright. Along the roads of your life, a protective shield has formed that both, holds out the things that scare you and holds tightly onto the things that you believe help you feel whole, loved, valued, and beautiful. Things that enable you to feel loved and loving.

The higher calling here for you, with your event and with this intention to heal, is your song of self-love and self-acceptance. Here are your inherent essential elements of your essence of love; patiently awaiting their bloom. Preparing for the opening to your heart soul channels; to run through the veins of your Being, with the healing sparkles of all your power; fearless compassion, in-love energy, expansive openness and a fierce awake heart - that authentic love embodies. Your essence is love. To open yourself to that awareness, to embrace the concept and to choose to see and engage all things from your essence is to become love; to embody love.

Darling, I agree that it sounds simple to say and seemingly hard to find. Especially when you are aching just to feel your old normal self again. I can hear you saying, "Come on! This feels really hard!" What you are journeying through is hard right now. All this other talk of higher "woo-woo" love might feel like too much. I know…I started out broken and feeling emotionally exhausted and beaten too.

Here's what I discovered. My old understanding of boundaries did not help me to stay safe. I soon discovered my boundaries were in dire need of deeper exploration. I asked, "What are boundaries?" How do you establish healthy boundaries when you are starting from scratch? And, what is the connection between healthy boundaries and my version of *BigLove*? Should I make my boundaries tighter, clearer, stronger? Where could I go from here with a broken heart, crappy boundary results, and a feeling that everyone but me had figured it out with their long "happy" marriages?

When my shield cracked open and light was able to escape out, the answer that it is all about love, became clearer to me. Self-Love. *BigLove.* When you open up to discover who *you* are, and you choose to transform your own view of Self, with a radical self-acceptance of your perfectly imperfect you – you invite this enlightening shift. Here is the doorway to a self-empowering, self-loving, self-accepting and enduring life romance, from which, your fierce, expansive and profoundly powerful capacity to love Self and others, is unlimited. This is not an overnight trip, girlfriend … it is a lifelong intention which transforms the quality of your life, moment to moment.

Boundaries you thought should be tight and solid, transform into boundaries that become powerful, expansive and inclusive. These are created from a source of loving in such a magnificent way that you no longer feel the need to hold things off from fear, but instead, to hold your heart open, *even* when it's scary, painful or hard. You are open-hearted with courage and the power of self-trust about what is for you and what is not. You know the difference between what enhances your loving life experience, and what you can continue loving, with forgiveness, but must part ways with, because it is not *for* you; like a love-energized line in the sand. You wish them well and continue to love those that are of a different relationship mind-set. While choosing self-love *more*, rather than, the self-sacrifice it would take, to stay in that connection.

How you love yourself clarifies your view of the challenge in front of you. Which is, how do you actually decide to stay with him, or to go? When you consider it from a self-view of unworthiness, you may ask yourself, "If I give up my husband, does that mean she wins? Do I really win if he stays? How do I win this? How do I know what to do?"

First, my darling, this is *not* a competition. It is a life experience and you have choice. Now, let's say you choose to think about the big decision from your grounded root of love, you may ask, "What would life be like without him? Do I see myself defined by him? How do I define myself for myself? Can I bear the thought of him not being here in the morning, anymore, when I open my eyes?" Clarity of heart and mind is so essential. When you know how powerful you are from your core essence of love, then you are empowering your own belief, that you truly have choice.

Choose to honestly look within, and ask yourself, whether the man and the marriage, is *for you*. Or, are you holding close something toxic. Choose to honestly feel your way into, whether your man is authentic and true, and whether it is his desire to be forgiven for the profound pain he has brought to you and your marriage. Consider whether he honestly demonstrates a deep commitment and willingness to seek the answers within himself; to his acted-out struggles; to access his own self-love, and to commit to the redesigning of an enduring renewed love for you, in all ways, and in your marriage.

This is the flavor of the feelings that we want after an event of betrayal. What we really, *really* want is some sort of guarantee. However, love is not a guarantee. Love has no guarantee to remain stable and last forever. It is a living, dynamic thing. It changes and evolves just like us. It can be strengthened and nurtured to deepen and grow. It is like a garden that must be tended to, because no matter how beautiful it starts out we are in it to love; reap love, replant love, and renew love even if it all burns away. And still there are no guarantees. Which is why we are called to be warriors of love; resilient and ever rising.

What is another powerful way that you experience the energy of love? One dimension, many lovely ladies find challenging (including myself) is allowing in the feeling of belonging. Belonging is a component of the energy of love. We all have the need to belong. Our challenge to believe that we belong, even when, the evidence offers room for various interpretations. Self-empowerment is ignited in the choice you choose to believe, because it creates or reinforces the meaning you already hold. The story you tell yourself. I do matter vs. I don't matter. Your view of your worthiness and lovability is reinforced by your strength of self-love. Your choice to deeply believe, accept, know, and feel the reinforced powerful sense of Self that says:

Yes! Yes!

You do *matter!*

You are a social Being. You need community. No woman (or man) is an island – this is a powerful truth. You began life birthed into a tribe, whether two-hundred large or two people small. You need to dedicate time cultivating your loving tribe of family and friends to allow happiness in. While at the same time, you also need space for solitude; to be with the quiet of your heart and mind; to allow and listen to what is going on deep inside of yourself. Embrace the healing of meditation, prayer, noticing your thoughts, beliefs, and meanings that you give to events, and to other's actions. Embrace the healing of allowing open space for curiosity; to seek understanding, rather than diminishing yourself through unchecked thoughts of unworthiness coming from within you. Embrace the healing in building self-awareness in the moments when you notice you are assigning meaning to other's actions, as self-imposed proof of your own unworthiness.

Exploring and developing a clear understanding of the view you hold of yourself, is vital and essential for your healing and *BigLove* journey. Your courage to weather the discouraging opinions that well-intended friends or family offer, out of love for you, about your event, will also feel challenging. While their concerned feedback is worthy of attention, it is in your courage to remain open to hear it and still hold to self-belief that you will know what is the right choice for you. Your strength will come from your centered self-love and compassion to stand firm with your choice and not to give up, yet.

To love another with healthy self-loving boundaries is a power that does not restrict but expands your capacity to *BigLove*. Exploration with the intention to understand the inclusiveness of *BigLove*, reveals that forgiveness is an essential element of *BigLove*. The paradox of love and forgiveness is that in the act of giving these to another, which on the surface may seem grand and generous of the giver, and of benefit only to the receiver, at closer look, we come to understand that the energy of both is the precious field of grace. This grace captures love's light and enhances the living experience of both beings. The receiver must be willing to open with vulnerability to accept forgiveness. This is only possible when their belief is acknowledging that something hurtful happened, which needs to be forgiven. Therein lies their potential to become the catalyst of a ripple of Grace, for as they receive grace the possibility increases for then to feel inspired to turn and offer grace to others. And in this divine reciprocity of love, you lay the foundation for your new relationship, marriage and love.

My dear friend, let me empower you with this insight: This "ripple of Grace" is regardless of whether you discover that your marriage and your man is a situation that doesn't enhance your life, or align with your self-love. If your best choice is to end the marriage, if you have discovered this is best for you … know that loving and forgiveness are still Grace for you to give and receive. This is the magic. The miracle of the event is that buried beneath the pain and heartbreak in your experience of betrayal, nothing – no matter how painful – is wasted.

Regardless of the courageous choices you make, what fuels self-love is that the decisions are given with and through compassion, love, and forgiveness. To choose to endeavor to remain open to all these life experiences allows the alchemy of heartbreak to transform into a wake-up to enlightenment of your soul. Like being birthed, we endure with instinct to survive the rough journey, hollering our way into this outer life; in this earthly experience. We slide into the vast expansive options that await us to choose how we will show up in every new event. All creating circumstances with new experiences requiring choices; opportunities to evolve; to the *you* that you are meant to *become*. While holding harmony in self-love, to accept that you are always enough, and perfectly imperfect, in your brilliant and beautiful humanness at any moment.

Love is an essential element for healing through forgiveness. The topic of love is truly endless and wonderous. My deepest desire with this chapter, my friend, is to clearly demonstrate that love is a precious muscle of energy which requires training, practice, discovery and focus. Your current view of love can evolve. It is meant to evolve. Practiced self-awareness requires intentional training to shift from disempowering thoughts toward those that lead to higher choices; by reframing to a different word or thought, meaning, or action. Repeating this creates self-empowering change within you. Neuroplasticity has proven you can change. You can powerfully evolve. I created a term for myself to help me to remember and stay connected to my higher goal; to choose from my essence of love, with self-love; moment to moment. A practice I fully admit is a daily training of intention to make a loving higher choice. It is a tender and self-loving reminder of who I am choosing to be and become, as I show up in my life and relationship – every day. My specially coined term, which you have already seen sprinkled on the pages of this book, my love letter to you – is *BigLove*. I think of it as an energy-calling from within my Being - to bring forth my most powerful state-of-Being from Love.

Dear heart, I offer it to you as a love-trick to use, as you go through your days and lean into the many conflicts, issues, and normal bumps that will come on this very courageous journey. Use it by asking yourself, from your most powerful magnificent state of *BigLove*, "What is the most loving, compassionate and gentle view I can hold for this?" And from there you can explore how you want to be love, embody love, and come from love; to respond to whatever comes on your path to healing. Now that you have dipped your toe in the exploration of *BigLove*, join me as we move toward a deeper understanding of the next essential element: forgiveness.

Chapter 5:

Your Rooted Queendom of Fierce Forgiveness

"There is a nobility in compassion, a beauty in empathy and a grace in forgiveness."
– John Connelly

"We have the tendency to want the other person to be a finished product while we give ourselves the grace to evolve."
– T. D. Jakes

A s a young girl, the second of five children, my older sister's cognitive disability moved me to first position in responsibility to keep us all on the right track. We had such scary consequences of discipline from our parents, for stepping out of line, that I became a vigilante against fun, silliness, or any sign of kid behavior that might go sideways and bring disaster down on all our heads. Mine was a full-time, joyless job. My younger sister was born full of silly-heart joy and lots of wild curiosity. These are qualities characteristic of natural joy in children, but which didn't work well in the environment we grew up in. As the years passed, I grew to dislike her and the way she always rebelled against all the rules that I had come to feel kept us safe. She didn't keep herself safe. She appeared recklessly fearless. I feared for her, and I resented the feelings of fear she brought up in me. I began to resent her.

Sharing a bedroom in our small home, we spent most of our youth in small quarters with large friction. My parent's style of pushing her onto me, to "straighten her out," even after I was first married, only made it worse. I held to my harsh fearful protective boundaries and attitudes, which I used against her in judgment. For most of my twenties, thirties, and forties, I didn't feel I knew, liked, or trusted her. I know now that I was angry with her for just being a kid while I, another kid, tried to control her. I held it all against her with my concrete sense of righteousness. Eventually in my mid-forties, during one of my efforts to help her financially, she (then in her early forties) and my young niece (a sweet seven) came to live with me and my (now ex-) husband. We bumped heads almost daily as my well-intended, old-patterned efforts continued to try to control her with my version of the "right path". One night, her chronic asthmatic condition got the best of her. It was very late, and she called an ambulance and was transported to the hospital ER, still in the early stages of a potentially life-threatening asthmatic attack. While in the ER, as the medical teams attempted to treat and stabilize her, the event escalated, and she suddenly began crashing. Her air cut off, she stopped breathing and had to be "code blue" resuscitated, and then was intubated.

I was completely unaware of this happening. I was back home, deeply asleep in bed. My niece had gone with her mom silently in the ambulance. At about 4 a.m., my niece phoned me to come.

By the time I finished talking with the doctors and was able to see my sister, I was shaken to the bone and so stoically angry with her. As I entered her room, I could see she was physically beaten down. Unable to speak, her eyes were wide as she lay, hands tied to the bed with a tube down her throat; frightened beyond words. Once she saw me, she seemed comforted, and closed her eyes.

As I sat next to her bed, and gently placed my hand on hers, the most amazing thing happened. I could feel the subtle increase of my body's vibration followed by an overwhelming sense of tender compassion for her. She looked so completely helpless and vulnerable. I felt grounded but connected and energetically linked to all her fear and her pain. I felt such complete loving empathy for her as though I *was* her. In that moment a very surreal sensation occurred. I could literally feel the anger *melting and running down my body*. It felt as if I was a lit candle stick and the melting wax was running down my sides. I began to weep as I filled with a profound and complete sense of love, compassion, and forgiveness, with all my Being, for the whole of who she was. I remember being overtaken with an energy of pure love, I would now say, my essence of love; *BigLove*. In that moment, I was aware that I had forgiven her. It was like all the hardness and anger had melted off me. *I felt released*.

My sister was still herself, but it was a different me who finally was able to see her differently. With my awareness of love and new openness, I was able to be loving and accepting of her. It changed everything. Something had changed in me, which from then on allowed me to express more loving boundaries with her. I became able to notice when judgment rose in me and endeavored to mindfully choose my responses. It awakened responses, with a new communication style that supported my healing and seemed underpinned by the forgiveness miracle that had occurred. To this day, I gratefully regard the devastating experience as *a miracle*. I believe I felt the miraculous energy of grace through forgiveness, and in the midst of it all, I rediscovered a sister who today, I consider one of my best friends.

So, what does the sharing of the story of my sister hold for you? I spent most of my young life and up into my forties feeling betrayed by, angry at, and full of judgment of my younger sister. I was a prisoner of the hard feelings I held against her. Feelings that sat in my energy like a big brick wall, blocking much of my access to joy and lightness in my heart. All without my awareness. I thought *she* was the problem. Until the day my heart softened and I allowed compassion, forgiveness and *BigLove* to begin healing my heart. There were decades of pain to heal. I had to courageously open and remain open to allow authentic healing through forgiveness, because she didn't change – I did. Then my view of my relationship with her did. Then she did. Forgiveness heals your life. Forgiveness is genuine love in action. It *is* Love. *BigLove*.

Come, let's explore Essential Element Number Three: Fierce Forgiveness. Forgiveness is not for the weak of heart. It is only for the very strong and is the only way to achieve peace of heart when one is wounded. To hold onto the anger and fear and pain is to put yourself in a cage with no escape from your own anger, fear and pain. Nelson Mandela, who suffered much in his remarkable life, said, "When a deep injury is done to us, we never heal until we forgive." A quotation by the Buddha states, "Holding onto anger is like drinking poison and expecting the other person to die."

Brave friend, when my guy betrayed me and broke my heart open, I already understood these powerful perspectives. I had spent time working on myself. I had knowledge of his previous relationship and their one little child. I practiced sending good energy and kind intentions to his child's mom for years. Even though I was aware of her hardness of heart, as demonstrated by patterned behavior, I believed sending good intentions would eventually heal her. I was "holding space" for us all to have the future chance for a cooperative and loving life forward; to make room for everyone. All good. Right? And, I was lovingly supporting my guy as he endured isolated living and working conditions. I was dedicatedly scheduling my time to be available most of the time for him on Skype. I was confident I had this under control.

So when the train of betrayal hit my relationship out of nowhere, I was completely devastated and cut off at the knees. My brain and heart halted. The big life challenging chess move had been made. Now what was I to do? I couldn't see my move. So, I got really quiet and listened. I waited for my heart to speak to me. After I worked through my grief, I realized I needed to pull myself up and begin rebuilding my strength. The one thing I knew is that *if* I wanted to remain in a relationship with him and for us to have a future love and life together (which I wasn't sure of yet), I would need to be very, very strong.

The paradox of forgiveness is that it is its own yin and yang. It requires profound strength and profound gentleness. You see, dearest, you might regard the act of forgiving as a show of weakness, a surrendering of your values, or a release of a call for justice in response to a deep wrong done to you. It's a letting go of the one place you feel powerful after your devastating experience of betrayal. You feel shielded with your heart's hardened conviction of righteousness. You feel powerfully in control. The door is closed and there is a big fat *no* on it. No forgiveness for you, buddy. However, that is not where your power is; it is in the courage and strength to be gentle, compassionate, kind, and willing to come from love, to do what love would do that ignites your true essence of power. Power from your essence of love. *BigLove.*

While I was writing this book, a lovely woman I've known for many years, who has similar challenges in her marriage, asked me what my book was going to be about.

"Forgiveness," I said. "Forgiveness after betrayal of an affair."

Her response was immediate, "Forgiveness isn't enough. It's not the answer."

I wasn't totally surprised. She is an intelligent, strong-willed, beautiful, professional woman who is led by her highly skilled intellect. But I sense she gets tangled up and hooked by her deep unresolved wounds and fears. The belief that forgiveness isn't enough, appears to be true, when you don't understand the vastness of what forgiveness is. From that view, it is judged too small to deal with the large journey of suffering you are hooked in. Thoughts of "I am right" feel like power. Holding onto the wound and denying forgiveness feels like power.

You're withholding something precious, that the person who injured you, desperately wants, in order, to make themselves feel better. To ease their suffering. Keeping that from them feels powerful. I wanted to mention this lovely woman's comment, because I had noticed that on this same day, I witnessed myself pull out my sword of righteousness during a disagreement with my guy. Attempting to make my high and mighty point, I swung it around with all my arrogant might. In hindsight, I could see that I got hooked by residual points of pain, and rather than graciously letting go of my point, I allowed it to drag me down the rabbit hole of history, lined with seeds of healing still trying to take root.

This made me wonder: am I not the same as my friend? I realized that forgiveness would take effort and stronger commitment to keep coming back to my intention, to come from love on my way to healing. The work of awakening is not for the faint. Returning to love and coming from love, both require soul grit, but the hardest part of all is in the brave willingness to soften and drop your walls even when fear of being vulnerable comes rushing back. All this power is energy from your deepest essence of love and love is more powerful than pride. This practice can get messy in your attempts to surrender, to feel vulnerable, then to catch yourself in pride's grip again. There are no guarantees around anything. There is power in choosing to accept yourself and your response. Self-acceptance enables validation that there's always a level of "okay-ness" in whatever you feel. You have a right to your feelings. Loving yourself allows you to see that you are not a victim. It opens the door to allow you to feel your power in compassion, to release you grip and open to letting go of your pain and anger.

In the movie *Sex and the City*, Miranda refuses to forgive her husband Steve for sleeping with another woman. He pleads for forgiveness and expresses his complete remorse for his mistake. He sends her flowers, letters, messages, he makes calls begging for forgiveness for six months. She remains emotionally closed, trapped in her cage of anger, pain, and punishment. At a rehearsal dinner for Carrie and Big, Miranda slips up and makes a comment to Big, which causes him to doubt his wedding with Carrie. With a full church, the wedding is stopped when Carrie is abandoned at the alter by Big. Paralyzed by his own fear, he can't get out of the limo. Devastated, Carrie feels completely humiliated. Miranda comes to suspect that she might have been the cause of this breakdown but is so afraid to confess to Carrie that she waits for three months to say anything. Finally confessing, a broken-hearted rage is re-ignited in Carrie as she responds to the shattering sense of betrayal by her close friend. She shouts, "I will never forgive you for ruining my marriage!"

Carrie stops talking to her. Miranda begs for forgiveness for weeks. Flowers, notes, calls, all asking for a chance to apologize for her careless, hurtful action that had a painful consequence for Carrie. Carrie, deeply wounded and angry, shuts Miranda out. A week later, finally able to find an opportunity to force a face-to-face with Carrie in a taxi cab, Miranda pleads for forgiveness. Carrie finally tells Miranda that she wonders how Miranda could expect her to forgive her in a few days, when Miranda hasn't been able to forgive Steve after six months. Miranda argues, "It's not the same." Carrie counters, "It's forgiveness." And the cab driver nods.

With my guy, I knew all the logical conditions that contributed to this event of betrayal. I could sense his suffering that surfaced in any interaction with his son's mom. I confess that I was not completely aware of the darker power of her character or the extent she would go to in order to get what she wanted. I felt betrayed by the universe. It was a while before I learned that the good intentions I send out for others - feed *my soul*. Until then I was disappointed that my good energy and intentions consistently transmitted to her appeared to have been powerless against her mean-spirited, narcissistic behavior.

I felt compassion and a tenderness for my guy and all the very difficult experiences he has had to live through in his life. He is a war veteran, career military, who had come back with lots of hard-lived life experiences which he still carried around with him like open wounds. There are physical and emotional traumas that he still needs releasing and spiritual healing around. I knew all that and most of all I knew I loved him. I wanted to be able to *see* my way to forgive him.

As I created my path for forgiving him, I realized that I had to forgive myself, first. To forgive myself for not knowing what I didn't know. To forgive myself for thinking that I had all the power to control everything and keep us all on track. To forgive myself for my own imperfections which seemed more illuminated in the light of this suffering. To forgive myself for letting myself feel that I was not enough. To forgive myself for thinking I was self-confident and independent only to realize I had created my world around my guy instead of around myself. I had to forgive myself for all the things in me that disappointed me about my life, and my path of love, and for being disappointed rather than impressed by my resilience.

I stripped myself naked and forgave myself. Then I began with love to search for who I really am at my essence of love and Being and to choose how I was going to reframe every-thing – for me. How I was going to come from love and be love for myself. The start of my power was to let in the reality that with this or any situation - I have choice.

Dear friend, what can you open-up with compassion to forgive in yourself? Why are you holding back self-accep-tance and love from yourself? Take some time here. Pause. Let yourself "feel into it" and then journal. You will discover so much about yourself as you let the thoughts that rise just be expressed with open gates. Then turn and see yourself – whole beautiful, imperfectly perfect, and complete. Wrap your arms around your shoulders or place your hand on your heart and simply say. I love you I forgive you. You can add your name. You can speak into a mirror. This may sound "woo-woo" but you have the power to love yourself. Little by little. It is the start. Your kindness and compassion will soften you toward forgiving your guy.

My guy and I went through many stages while we practiced forgiveness with each other. For a long time, my words seemed detached from my body. I stayed convinced that he needed to show more remorse and he needed to demonstrate whatever would be a "sign" that he was sorry, over and over. I believed I had all the answers. I had read tons of books about getting in touch with our higher Self, in the collective consciousness and the power of everything. I had forgiven my sister and my parents, ex-husbands, family, friends … all for the various tiny to large levels of hurt or betrayal I had perceived them to do to me. I had studied how to communicate, when communicat-ing wasn't enough, how to meditate, and how to stay with the pain. I thought I had all the answers. Ha! All my answers were being sabotaged by my inability to practice living the answers I was getting to these questions: How would love do this? How would forgiveness do this? What would I be saying or doing if I really was forgiving him?

I continued to communicate my needs and wants to my guy. We fell into a pattern of too much talking about it and then no talking about it. We searched for the place to rest with each other. My truth is, it was all very hard. I would feel tender, and close. Then I would harden and shut down. We both felt alone and disconnected. I wanted him near, then I wanted him away. I could feel the pain of my open wounds and I wanted him to take them away.

My healing breakthrough came with I finally realized, that I had to stop treating him like he was getting close but was not quite worthy *yet* of my full forgiveness and respect. He told me he wasn't sure if he could ever be truly worthy again. Worthy enough for me to fully stop treating him like he was guilty and bad. I didn't realize I was treating him like he was guilty or bad. I could have argued against his perspective.

But what I was clear as a bell about was that I had some power that I was using in an anti-productive and unloving manner. I wanted a man who would feel my forgiveness, not just my lips moving. I wanted him to feel loved and safe with me. I wanted this for myself too, and I knew that unless I gave it to myself and allowed him to feel the warmth and love of it – we would never know if happiness was possible again. As I began to hold myself accountable for my softness, my loving tenderness, my kindness, my generosity of spirit and respect without asking him to qualify for it, our relationship changed. It didn't happen overnight. It happened over several years. I remember one day earlier this year sensing so clearly that the rock had lifted off my heart. The feeling in our relationship opened back up to love and to being in-love, with ourselves and each other. I could feel an ease of spirit, in our self-forgiveness, unfolding. It took a lot of practice and commitment and recommitment and a fearless awareness that if it wasn't going to ever be a good relationship again, that I was strong enough and self-loving enough to handle it. Only when we surrender our grip on the things we fear losing do we finally feel sufficiently liberated to love openly and completely if they stay. Conversely, if they go then our choice to deal with it from love remains and our courage to gratefully accept that life forward is still there *for* us to discover.

In the movie *Moonstruck*, Rose Castorini, a middle-aged, wise, and gentle, stay-at-home wife and mom, is searching to understand why men cheat. She is disappointedly aware that her middle-aged small business owner husband is having an affair with his secretary. During the movie she asks a number of different men, "Why do men chase women?" The answer that she finally accepts as the true answer to the question is "because they are afraid of dying." It was like the light switched-on in her head and she finally understood. Late that night, as her husband finally arrived home, she tells him, "I want you to know no matter what you do, you're gonna die. Just like everyone else!"

My initial plan was to offer some studies as to why partners cheat so that you might gain some understanding about it. I found many studies, articles, and loads of reasons. You can easily do that research on your own. My experience whispered to me a reminder that what will serve you is to understand what I learned that helped me.

I learned there are a thousand reasons that we can each find to justify a moment or a time of unfaithfulness. So, understanding the reason after it has happened, and needing to dissect it into pieces and nail all the windows of your relationship shut with really big, big nails is not going to stop it. Nor is it going to be a part of the healing process.

Here is what will. First, as I have said repeatedly, sweet lady, you are not to blame for his behavior. Second, *if* you and your husband are truly committed to healing your marriage and transforming it into a strong and beautiful partnership for your future together, then you must regard and have respect that attention to your relationship must become a priority. This effort is not to be considered a chore or a burden, but rather as a cherished dynamic priority that must be given attention with love. See this event of infidelity, which is one of the most devastating for a relationship to go through and survive, as a 911 wake-up call. Commit to explore it with each other all the parts that you each believe contributed to this event. Explore it without judgment, defense, justification or score. Simply practice listening and hearing each other. Practice mindfully speaking in soft and kind tones when you do engage in this communication. It makes a difference. Imagine you are visiting each other in a hospital and you want the other to hear your communication of love and comfort. Speak with that intention.

Differing views are not wrong or off limits. There is a time for that. The motivation behind the soft tone conversation is to intentionally create a safe space to get curious and listen to each other so that love can show-up and hear the places you can both come together and begin creating a more solid understanding and appreciation of your relationship and each other.

It is time to unlearn your old marriage, examine broken patterns and together envision and create your new, more engaged, loving re-commitment to your marriage.

If there is a lot of deep and painful unresolved emotional baggage that your partner has, or other issues that need to be untangled, explored and brought out for some sun and healing, then perhaps a relationship coach, or marriage therapist, or both, is a good place to explore. This book is not meant to have all the answers. You may be able to move forward with just what's here. What I do know is that this process is practiced best when you engage support from skilled others. The biggest mistake is to try to forgive, while ignoring what this event of infidelity is trying to communicate to you.

Dear beauty, although no one ever wishes this on anyone else, it has happened, so to reframe its purpose and see that this has brought you an opportunity to explore a higher consciousness around yourself, your marriage and your partner. Ignite the alchemy to transform your pain into forgiveness, authentic commitment and deeper love. On my path to healing, I discovered some rituals that were remarkably healing. I wanted to share a few as I end this chapter.

Healing Rituals on the Way to Letting Go

ᴄꙅ Find something of nature (a rock, twig, shell, wood) and write a word that means "forgiveness/letting go" to you on it. Go to the ocean and at sunset with some supportive girlfriends or alone. Create a loving forgiving intention in your mind. Hold it. Breathe into it and when you are ready to give it away – toss it way out into the ocean. Feel yourself agreeing to let it go.

Repeat this ritual as many times as needed to practice letting go.

ଔ Post inspiring quotes you can get off the internet which capture the feeling and attitude of forgiveness and love, compassion, and grace and any other qualities you want to practice with. Post them where you will see them with frequency. For example: Put them on your phone.

ଔ In the notes section of your phone, learn how to jot thoughts there. Whether you are out on the go or at your first wake-up, if you become aware that you are reflecting on your healing, or anything else that is about this healing path, no matter what the feelings or thoughts, be kind to yourself and let your finger tap out words into your phone. Empty your thoughts out, ease your monkey mind and capture your stream of consciousness. Later, when you have time re-read it and journal on it. Ask yourself: What were my thoughts trying to express? What were the feeling behind my thoughts? How can I practice coming from love with this? No right or wrong. Just get curious. There is healing in the act of listening with compassion to yourself.

ଔ Hire a coach for yourself. Explore this option if you sense a benefit of support is needed from someone who can provide a safe space of non-judgment to help you discover your own beauty and strength and wisdom in the midst of this life-changing path to healing. I am a coach and I have a coach and my coach has a coach, as all helping professionals should. On the Thank You page later in this book, you can find some support options from me.

ɔʒ Listen to how you talk about this within your social community. Choosing to speak with an intentional limit of reveal, is especially important as you are healing. Notice your tone and choice of characterization of the event. It all matters. Having good supportive friends is vital. Picking your inner confidant circle is as well. In Chapter 8, Showing up for Yourself, I will guide you on choosing with whom, and when, and how to share.

ɔʒ Choose a daily practice that helps you stay intentional with healing. Meditation, exercise, a mantra, post notes, play a special morning song, sing, have a friend call, choose a new morning greeting with your husband, pay attention to your smile frequency, and invite yourself to smile for no reason. It all adds up.

OK, lovely, get ready to light up as we move on to our next chapter and check out your untapped super powers. It's the perfect time to ignite them.

Chapter 6:

U R Awesome

*"...watching "hurt locker" right now...just so u
know...U.R. more awesome than the woman who
directed it will ever be... Your ability to be everything
for us all is better than any movie...i love u"*
– a text to me by my son, Lucas in 2010 (in response to my
expression of awe of Kathryn Bigelow the first woman to win
best director award for "Hurt Locker" at the 2010 Oscars.)

Amazing Super heart, it is time to explore, imagine and ignite your powers for this very challenging heart mission. Here is your 411 with Essential Element Number Four – Your Super Powers.

My last marriage, in my mind was going to be my last marriage. Three marriages felt like a lot for me to hold my head up with, at the time, but I had fallen in love with a fascinating, quirky, handsome, and kind man. I believed our five years of dating and testing the waters before we jumped in had done the trick. I believed happiness was mine. In hindsight (which is always clearer) I ignored some signs of a deeper, more complex nature that he showed every once in a while, so I accepted that as my choice. Along with all that I considered his wonderfulness, he also possessed an equally complicated, difficult deeper inner struggle, for me to deal with. I loved him and that was all I felt I needed. Our marriage had a long list of very hard times and challenges just like anyone's. Our marriage in our first year, endured and survived the death of his beautiful oldest son. This loss ignited harsh times to deal with, still I was going to make this work.

There are a million reasons behind why best-intentioned marriages don't work. In my last marriage it can be captured in one phase – there came a time when I didn't feel safe anymore. I had been working hard on my own contribution to this marital situation, long before I arrived at my place of personal clarity. Long before I realized, that for me to "want" to live, and be happy, I would have to leave. But before that clarity, I engaged directly and consistently to resolve our issues, which over time resulted in outcomes that forced me to find other options for coping. Remember, I was determined to stay. I had privately made a pact with myself that no matter what – I had made my bed and now I would die in it. I was committed to stay to my death in this marriage.

I was a strong, intelligent, fun, and funny woman. I was creative and sensitive. I found lots of ways to distract myself from my unhappiness. This included making myself lean into optimism and positivity to a fault. I also believed I had power. I could will myself to be happy and will myself to endure whatever came. I was powerful. For the last sixteen of almost nineteen years of our marriage, I tried hard to be happy enough. I was a sunny-side-up woman-girl so I always looked for ways to be happy.

During the last couple of years, I began noticing how much I was drinking. I hadn't been a drinker. I didn't really like to drink. But as years passed and things happened, something began to change in me. I was now looking for escapes and drinking was an easy social one. No one really noticed. I seemed as engaged as ever and my suffering was easy to cover up. With lots of friends and family, I was in touch with them, but most lived a distance from us. So I felt a bit isolated. Still, I endeavored to keep up a consistent "the show must go on" attitude, whenever I felt down. In the last few years of my marriage, despite years of couple's therapy, it became harder to contain my sadness and to carry on in life. I didn't feel loved or valued.

Eventually I had to "go dark" and stayed home more and more. I have two sons – men, really. Beautiful sons from my first marriage. We have a close, dynamic and complex relationship with each other, whether making each other laugh, needing support, or dealing with disagreement; we jump in and deal with it.

During the last two years, well before I made my decision to end my marriage, I had committed to try to take back the reigns for my happiness. Initially I demonstrated this by choosing to only invite people I enjoyed being with to share special events with me, and by this time unfortunately, that didn't include my husband. My birthday had arrived and I was entering my fifty-seventh year of life. I decided to ask my sons to join me for a day in the City. We could go to a museum and then have lunch.

It would be fabulous. It would be just the three of us. Our Saturday started out great, and I was so happy to be with my sons. Following the museum, we headed to downtown San Francisco and stopped into a pub for a drink. A friend of my son's showed up and joined us. One drink led to another and soon the night was completely submerged in alcohol. Now, don't judge my sons, I didn't expect them to police my drinks. They took care of me while I made my own choice to drink enough to get totally trashed. I could have stopped, but I chose to ignore my own self-care awareness and go for broke. My husband came to pick us up and drove us all home. While the alcohol processed through me, I lay in bed suffering for the next four days. I believe to this day that I almost died of alcohol poisoning.

On the first day that I could see well enough to write, I journaled a message to myself. I forgave myself for giving into the sadness and self-punishment. Then I asked myself if my example was the mom that I wanted my boys to know as a woman? And I made a pact to stop drinking to escape, and to find a way, if I was going to stay, to create a happy place in my head to truly be happy from. Essentially to be responsible for creating my own happiness.

As I healed from the self-abuse birthday episode, I asked myself, *"What is the most romantic and beautiful memory of love that you can remember?"*

And just like that, my heart pulled-up from the back of its lovely closet, my memory from high school of my guy. I thought, "Of course! This is a beautiful memory!" So, off I went and dug through my boxes of memorabilia, and finally found one thin purple Hallmark book signed by him with a sweet brief note, two tiny notes of a few sentences about civic text books, and a 3x2" high school senior picture with his note on the back. Having had no contact with him since graduation, I thought that this was the magic. Nothing had tarnished his memory so it was the perfect place to create my dream world. I simply made up a scenario that made me feel happy. Each night before I went to sleep, I would glide my fingers over the deep indents on the page with his inked words, read the little book and the few little notes he had written to me, then I would drop off to sleep hoping to dream from this loving space.

What happened over time was that I began to feel happier. I still had the same life, the same struggles and disappointments but I felt happier. I chose what I wanted to do and felt less sad about my loneliness. It didn't help me connect more in my marriage, but it helped me to compassionately tolerate our disconnect. This became my practice for eight months. People noted I seemed happier. I told them I had found my happy place.

In the ninth month of my happy place, during a medical exam to treat my abdominal aches, a discovery, prompting follow-on tests that eventually ruled out cancer, indicated instead that a hysterectomy was needed. *I considered it a brush with death and it woke me* up! I decided that after the scheduled surgery and a little time to recover I would request a divorce. Like my own personal version of Scarlett O'Hara, I raised my fist to the sky and said, *"I'll never give up again!"* I committed to start living my life for real. I immediately asked my husband to begin sleeping in the guest room. I told him it was because I was ill and needed my space. He graciously agreed to my request, which I was grateful for. I was not prepared to deal with disclosing my intention to divorce, until I had the overall strength to manage his response. I didn't want to provoke arguments of any type while I needed the home base to deal with my medical situation.

One month before my scheduled operation, I received a Facebook friend request. I was blown out of my chair to see that it was from the leading man of my happy place dream, my high school secret-love – my guy. I casually welcomed the old friend connection and had no reason to believe that it was anything other than just that. I hadn't spoken to him in forty years. We began emailing and sharing the stories of our lives ... and the rest is history, as they say.

My dear friend, you may be wondering, did I make that happen? Did I manifest the dreams I created? I don't know. But whether I did or not, it wasn't a guarantee of happiness ever-after, with no dark times. (Obviously, right?) It was still life and whatever I was going to make of it. I was building resilience. What I do know is *you* are powerful. Your thoughts and energy make things happen. You are living the consequences and events that have come to you. Choose to come with your power. Choose to build resilience. A powerful question to ask in any hard moment is: "In the midst of what is here, what is the most powerful state of mind I can live it in?" Listen for your heart's answer. It will come. Let's look at some more super power examples.

In 1968, when I was fifteen, an episode of *Star Trek* captured my heart forever. It was titled "The Empath." It was basically a story of a captured member of an empath species, her name was Gem. Held in a lab by another species Vian to study her empathic capabilities and their development. They captured Kirk, Spock, and McCoy and inflicted suffering on them to observe and track how the empath would respond. My friend, it is a beautiful episode, easily found on the internet. Treat yourself to it.

As I watched the story of this lovely, kind, compassionate, gentle, curious, courageous, and frightened empath and her capabilities unfold, I felt like I was watching the answer to "who am I?" being played out in front of me. Her story of taking on others pain into herself and then healing them and herself – was what I believed my highly sensitive, empathetic, intuitive, aware, compassionate, and determined energy was to be used for. As a child I could hear, see, feel, absorb – everything. Much more than a child is equipped to handle. I felt myself suffering because of it but I didn't know how to deal with it. The good news is *The Empath* gave me a way to *see* what I was feeling. The big downside was that it instilled a thought that I was supposed to take on other people's hurts, wounds, pain, and absorb it and heal them and myself. Which turned out to be a very poor foundation for creating healthy loving boundaries.

The beauty in this story of Gem is her super powers are her capacity to engage on a high level with the qualities that make us all Human. These qualities include kindness, compassion, love, empathy, understanding, intuition, suffering, forgiveness, joy, engagement, courage, fear, anger, patience, and more. Every emotion that you can think of is energy in motion. You have intuitive hits about things. You sense someone is happy or sad. You can feel when your kid isn't quite right. Those are your powers lighting up and engaging. To the degree that you choose to pay attention to developing your powers will determine the degree to which they will develop for your life. When you see yourself as capable of expansive love *–BigLove –* and you practice ways to engage development of them, you begin to feel more in touch with the powers that are your inheritance.

Ten years ago, through some friends I met, I was introduced to Reiki. I had never heard of Reiki. Once introduced, I was hooked. I began going to an amazing practitioner for regular sessions, where she combined the healing modalities of Reiki and acupuncture. Soon I found my way to attend training to learn the practice of Reiki healing. I read *the* book on Chakras, *Wheels of Life* by Dr. Judith, about our energy centers. I finally felt I had come to an understanding with, and found a home for, my empathic abilities and healing. At http://greenlotus.hubpages.com/hub/Reiki_Really_Works-A_Groundbreaking_Scientific_Study you can read a brief paper on proof that Reiki works. (If you are unfamiliar with Reiki this study is a great introduction.)

So, what is this proving? The message for you and me, dear one, is that these powers are in us. *In You.* While I was in my training class for Reiki, the class engaged in a practice of distance healing. Our group of twenty each picked a partner. We spread out all over the very large room. Turned our chairs so that we were not facing each other. Lights out, shades pulled shut, and eyes closed. Our assignment was to practice energetically sending healing to our partner across the room. The receiving student was to relax and be open to receive. Then we were to switch roles. We had learned the proper Reiki igniting terms and the path of where to place our hands in a basic healing session when the client is laying in front of you. From our chairs, we were to do this in our mind envisioning the practice as we had been trained. We began and were in practice for fifteen to twenty minutes.

As a beginner student, I didn't have expectations that I would be remarkable or stupendous, right off the bat, but here's what my partner reported. He felt the heat of my energy start at the top of his head and move to his face. But then, instead of moving down his body, as we are normally trained to do, he became aware of the heat energy focused on his legs. He reported gratitude for this, because his legs had been aching him all afternoon. After the practice, he said, his legs felt more relaxed. I was stunned into silence. He had felt my healing energy from across the room. You see, my friend, I had started my Reiki exercise, in my mind, beginning at his top of head as he reported, and after moving to his neck area, I felt intuitively pulled to focus my healing energy to his legs. A sense of intuitive direction I didn't question, but simply followed. The class reinforced my belief in our inherent powers. I left that training with a new vibration awakened in my body and my Being. An unearthed awareness that I am a woman with super powers and that day they were ignited.

In the book *Green Mile* by Stephen King, John Coffey was a supernatural empath. He was a massively huge, gentle soul of a man. He was capable of extraordinary healing and empathy. Mr. King's story illustrates themes of the super powers we have with the power of love, compassion, and healing. John Coffey's innocence and suffering that he endured because of his abilities beautifully illustrates that our super powers can be our gift as well as our curse.

The supernatural door that I want to invite you to open to support and love yourself in this very challenging time of healing is the door called Joyful Curiosity.

Become curious about your own gifts and talents – your powers. Explore how you can ignite in your day, in your marriage with joy, kindness, gratitude, laughter, optimism, gentle energy, truth, love, compassion, and healing.

Reengaging in intimacy after your "event" is a process with no time line. There is no rush. Things have been broken that must be cleared and rebuilt. This takes time. The intentional task in front of you and your husband is to explore together and create understanding about what intimacy is to each of you, now. What will you both, or individually need, in order to feel enough trust, closeness, safety, tenderness and freedom to be intimate again? You might start with an easy intention, like creating a plan for a sweet afternoon to just lie in bed and talk. To lie with each other, in each other's arms. With loving agreement and willingness to be OK with nothing more until each is ready. This can feel very hard. One may be ready before the other. It is in the practice of giving with this beautiful generosity, that you will begin to lay the new foundation for intimacy. When you feel safe again you will know what to do. Until you are ready to get really close perhaps creating an intention for you and your man to lay new seeds of desire is enough. What would that look like for you? Ask each other. One idea, that might seem crazy but is fun, is to practice sitting across from each other and engaging in a five-minute gaze of love practice. Just silently gaze into each other's eyes with intentional thoughts to only see the other's beauty, strength, and light. Sometimes all this creates is a lot of laughter. But don't discount laughter … it can be a powerful seed toward building a loving connection. If sexual intimacy just doesn't feel like it is comfortable yet, don't judge it; we all heal at our own pace. Have courage and practice kindness, compassion and patience with each other. You could try to invite your husband to create a dream scenario with you where you are both the romantic leads in your own story. Talk about it. Write it. Play with it. Words are powerful. Thoughts are powerful. Emotions build from the seeds you plant.

Beauty, here is the super power seed I most want to plant with you in this chapter. Stand in your wisdom and know that you are just as super human, gifted, amazing and talented … as I am. We each have our soulful beauty, powers, and journey to shine and thrive in. Let's reflect the magic of each other like mirrors of love. Your power increases as you embrace love from your chosen tribe of loving women and radiate love out to them, in loving reciprocity. We can heal each other. While researching the term Queendom, I came across a 2006 video moment with "Queen" Jill Scott while she was waiting for her turn to perform on stage for the Dave Chappelle Block Party Show. She was listening with admiration to the female singer performing at the time. When asked if she was nervous or intimidated to go on after the brilliance of the last performer, she gracefully laughed and said, *"We all have our own thing. That's the magic. And everybody comes from their own sense of strength, their own Queendom. Mine could never compare to hers, and hers could never compare to mine."* She is beautifully strong, confident and gracefully generous with capacity to see the beauty, strength and awesomeness of other women too. Confident women do *not* compare or compete with other confident women. They build each other up. Queen Jill Scott models a powerful confident woman.

What's your power? Find it. Self-actualize with it. Become the you that you're meant to be. Be confident. It is your super power to ignite. Live it. Own it.

Now that your super powers are sparking, let move on to expand the view of your world.

Chapter 7:

Your Magical Unicorn Perspective

"We are all in the gutter, but some of us are looking at the stars."
– Oscar Wilde

Let's polish up your lens as we focus on Essential Element Number Five – Perspective.

Quite a number of years ago, I traveled to the spectacular city of Tbilisi in the Republic of Georgia for a few weeks. My guy was working there. In this post-Soviet republic, the resilient and serious Georgians had endured hard political knocks. The tone of the community in the aftermath of the Soviet Union was reflected in the monochrome palette of cultural fashion of dark brown and black colors, bustling on the streets on any workday. A tone mirrored on the tired and run-down facades on residential multi-level buildings, that lined the blocks. Tbilisi is an amazing place of gorgeous history, and its people, especially the young are wonderfully friendly and engaging. As Americans, there were times we were treated like celebrities. Young Georgians hearing us speak English would ask to have their picture taken with us. It was a hoot. I am happy to say I made many friends there, and am still in contact with a few precious beauties, especially through Facebook.

During one particularly unforgettable night, my guy and I ventured out for a stroll in the market area. The sun was rolling down the sky, as the older street lamps flicked on, demonstrating their limited reach of light. Pedestrians were rushing about in the distance. They were softly lit, roaming images who crisscrossed traffic full of buzzing youth and couples. People who, just like us, had come out to enjoy some street food and peruse trinkets displayed in the tattered old kiosks that lined the road.

As we strolled up the sidewalk on this slightly up-hilled street, I could see up ahead on the crest. Darkened silhouettes of folks back-lit by headlights headed in our direction, whose shadows reflected onto the shiny rainy street, from an earlier pour. We walked along hand in hand, low key as possible, offering respect to the local custom of legally limited public displays of affection. It was a magical evening. Our plan was to walk and take in this fascinating culture then to head over to an Indian restaurant we had made reservations with.

We were just about at the crest of the road and I spotted what looked like a group of five young people, who I guessed were between the ages of eighteen to twenty-two. What hooked my attention was a little dog. Think of a small Jack Russell Terrier. The dog looked thin and a bit skiddish, as though all the noises and energies of this street had him on overload. What caught my eye, as we walked closer to the group to pass, was the dog was being held by a rope tied around his neck. I am profoundly distressed by this practice. It triggers my tears, even now to think of it. And then, as we walked closer to pass, close enough to see them, the dog paused and turned to look right at me. His eyes and mine locked and for what realistically, was about ten seconds, but seemed like five minutes. All I could see, and sense, was sadness and suffering. I didn't stop to pet him because the group was giving off vibes of the Sid Vicious and Nancy Spungen sort; punk, sharp, edgy, unfriendly. I didn't want to make it worse for the dog. I suddenly felt panic. My strategic mind zoomed into savior mode and my monkey mind threw every thought of "save the *dog!*" that it could muster. I turned to my guy and whispered, "Oh my gosh Babe." He didn't understand what had grabbed me. He held my hand tighter and we turned to go back down the hill. I passed the dog again and gave it my all to send love to him. We continued quickly down the hill away from the dog and his master.

Not more than a minute later, I heard the cry of a wounded animal. I spun around and looked up the hill to see the silhouette of my canine friend being kicked by the master shouting stupid dog phrases for his wandering nearer the street. The sound and sight locked my heart in a vice and I told my guy I had to do something. He held me and said calmly, "We are in another country. They do not have protective laws for dogs. If you cause a problem, you will be sent home, and that is all that will happen." I felt like someone was holding me under the water. I said. "Okay."

And then I ran. Away from the place of pain. I ran and ran. I realized I didn't know where I was going and better stop. Then I remembered my Pema Chodron guided Tonglen meditation training. I stopped and found a place to sit. For the next twenty minutes, I repeated a meditation sending wishes for freedom from suffering and the root of all suffering to my canine friend, to his master and to myself. I inhaled in the pain and suffering, and I breathed out loving intentions for healing and forgiveness. I just stayed with the pain and I repeated the meditation prayer over and over. At the very end I asked God, the Universe, Loving Source, and all angels and powerful Beings to please let the dog's misery end. Even if that meant his death. It would be a few days before I could completely unhook from the event's trauma, but the Tonglen medication felt like powerful medicine when I needed it. And I had the power to help myself with me all along. I believed and still believe we affect the world with our words, intentions and the energy that we put out there. We have a very big responsibility to choose well.

My loving friend, your perspective on any situation is a power game changer. My intention in sharing the above story was to demonstrate that suffering is everywhere. What we do with it, how we view it, and how we work with it is where the golden juice for self-love, self-empowerment, self-acceptance and *BigLove* reside. When you can stay with your suffering, your processing of grief, or anger, or when the triggers pop-up and jab you, you will be able to acknowledge, stay open, be ready to work with them, toward your healing. When you can do this, you will be maximizing your super powers and practicing with your power of profound love. Each time you engage in these practices you will grow stronger and feel energetically larger. Your energy of love will fill the room as it radiates from your body. You will be waking up and expressing your whole beautiful you. As Glinda in *The Wizard of Oz* told Dorothy,

"You've always had the power to go home … you had to learn it for yourself."

Practicing intentional work around love and forgiveness and compassion will enhance your perspective and empower it with a courage you never knew you had.

With his action, my guy created a turbo-super-sized, life-long consequence for our lives. I had to wrap my head around a million different ways to see this so that I could accept it, heal it, integrate it into my life, and become comfortable with it. In my effort to come from love, while I was still in the shock of it all, I even agreed to try to reach out and create a bridge between the mother and I, so we could all try to be a family of cooperative parents. After all, because she had had to locate donor eggs and have them fertilized with my guy's hijacked sperm and then have them implanted in her, all to make this very complex covert operation occur – I believed and still believe they are my children as well, since they were created essentially from my guy, during our relationship. I found it quite interesting when someone recently said, that they can understand why my guy did what he did. "At least he didn't sleep with her," they innocently added. This is true. What is also true is that with knowledge of all the lies, denials, allowances, and suppression of my own intuition, for a long time, it literally felt like she had raped and robbed *me*. In the end, regardless of my most genuine and kind efforts to connect with her, she remained consistent with her nature of mean-spirited manipulation, even with me. So, I finally stopped, stood up and began showing-up with strong and fair healthy boundaries. I began to establish my voice about *how* my guy and I would engage with her. Plus most importantly, we got very legal and clean about establishing how our future would look. We still have a ways to go and lots of pieces to this puzzle to solve, but we have the rest of our lives to get into a good rhythm with it all.

Broaden Your Lens

We all see things through the filters we have developed in our lives. So, understanding this and choosing to widen our lens so that we can hold a more expansive space in which to view our circumstances allows our generosity of spirit and forgiveness and understanding to expand as well. Let's look at a few examples of movies that demonstrate the power of perspective.

In the movie, based on the book *Life of Pi* by Yann Martel, a profound story of healing after tragedy is told. After their zoo in India struggles, a young man and his family endure the ocean trip to Canada with their animals. During it all, the ship which is transporting some of their animals to be sold in North America sinks. Some die and some are put out on lifeboats to try to survive. The story is from the perspective of the young man and his journey on a lifeboat with a tiger. I don't want to ruin the story for you if you have not read or watched it, but I encourage you to do just that. What brings meaning for you, my dear, is that the boy in the story turned everything into something positive. The pain, the death, the loss, the struggle, and even the perspective of how it all really happened. Everything that happened on his journey, was given value and purpose, in the story he recalled. He saw himself as the strong resourceful survivor. He told his story of struggle from a point of courage, compassion and resilience. His depiction of the event demonstrated him to be a hero of his story and not, as many believed, a victim.

In the movie *Unfaithful*, the story is told of a happily married middle-aged comfortable family living the good life in suburbs of New York. By a chance of fate, the wife, Connie is seduced by this new charming, mysterious and risky stranger, who ignites all the parts of her that had gone to sleep in her predictable life. The affair becomes her obsession. Her husband Edward digs deep to uncover all the details her infidelity. Edward, driven and tortured by this discovery goes to confront her lover and is ignited into a level of rage that he could never have imagined. The actions that result bring unimaginable consequences that forever change the trajectory of their world. The tragedy of this story is that the act of infidelity drove everyone so insane, that not even their seemingly solid life up to that point could protect them from seeking revenge and spinning completely out of control. They lost their way and failed to employ the love they felt between them as a way to survive beyond this event of betrayal.

My friend, whether you are a movie fan, a reader, an internet surfer, my experience has shown me that searching for stories, movies or anything inspiring or revealing, that opens your lens to see and feel a similar experience is helpful and cathartic. To see someone else make a huge error of judgment in how they handle their response to a "thing" you are going through can many times help widen your perspective of how you want to be. Even the movie *The Help* so beautifully shows a variety of responses that were chosen by Skeeter's mom once she realized it was time for her to finally stand up to the bigotry that her daughter so courageously wrote about to help the maids have their voices heard. Skeeter wrote to expose the injustices from an energy of love, compassion, and righteous decency.

She used the power she had to reveal the wrongs, discover her voice, and employ the power of her pen.

A New Kind of Noticing

What kind of detective do you want to become from this event? Oh, it is perfectly natural to start off when your trust has been broken, with nothing but suspicion about everything. You become hypervigilant around everything looking for signs and indicators that the man who broke your heart is lying, though he has said he was sorry and wants to stay. And if he isn't lying he soon will be because now you have labeled him a liar. Well, first let me tell you, you will stay very busy, very alert and get very weary. Your skills of noticing will become so sharp that you will notice things that aren't even there to notice. As well as, things that were there all along, that you never noticed before, because they weren't important to notice. You will make a list of everything; that you need him to sign in and out about. Check and double check where he is and what he's doing. Lock down the windows and doors. You can keep everything safe, tight, and protected. You might realize things really aren't safe, but now you are on watch. You feel in control. That's what happens when you dial in the focus and believe your life, your marriage, and everything depends on how well you keep watch. Whew! Egad! This is a prison sentence and you have locked yourself in a cage. There you are being slowly eaten by the green-eyed monster named Jealousy, who has tossed the key off the cliff into the ocean. Oh no! This is not what I want for you!

Okay, my sweet, lovely friend. Let's start over. How 'bout you imagine this? You are a Love Detective. What does this mean? Your intentional focus is on the beauty of each day. You dial-in to look mainly for the good, the gold and the silver-linings in everything. You practice optimistic views, positivity and acceptance. You play the happy game, in which you decide to intentionally try to find the upside of everything. (Add the song "Happy" by Pharrell Williams as background music). Look for the synchronicities that make something that seems impossible possible. I practice this all the time, but it really served me when my guy and I had to manage time to see the kids and deal with the inconsiderate shenanigans of their mom. My list read: "Synchronistic Moments: 1) Early delivery of babies 2) Preemie-Babies in NICU 3) No rooms at Marriott proper 4) Residence INN full but sudden cancellation 5) Severe snow creates Room for us 6) Her sudden change of child visit times gives us an opportunity to find an attorney. 7) Her change of time again, forces us to miss attorney appointment, which creates time to receive update on my guy's job and choose a better lawyer."

Each one of these points at the time they were happening, seemed like the worst hurdles and they just kept coming. It wasn't until some quiet time came and I relaxed to process all that had been happening with a mind for looking for the good and upside of it all – that these floated to the top. I jotted them down in my little notebook and reviewed them like a fairy dipping her toes in a magic pond. I could see the power of the Universe holding my back. I had decided to take on this challenge of healing and it was a doozy. But what this list told me is that I am not alone. There is a larger force of love and life energy that is with me. I took it as a sign of reassurance that the *force* is indeed with me. Well my dear – the same energy of love and life force is supporting you. You are not alone. There is a mighty force with you.

My daughter-in-law is a lovely gal. She is smart and creative, and she loves my son. This makes me happy. She is not a talker, or a chatterbox like I can be when I get wound-up. She measures her words and can appear rather serious and quietly controlled in a way that sometimes causes me to wonder if all is okay. And it is…she is just low-key, self-contained. One day out of the blue I received a package from her. Delightfully surprised, I opened it and found she had sent me a mellow-yellow T-Shirt silkscreened with the name Leon in blue letters. This itself was a joy, because Leon is my maiden name, which I had recently returned myself back to, from the history of all my previous names. I felt it was akin to me rising from the ashes for myself, if you will. And then I opened the card. A white card with one phrase on the front, printed in letters outlined in a thin black line, colored in with a progression, of bright pink to light pink. The phrase said, "YOU ARE A MAGICAL UNICORN." She noted inside that she had seen "this" and thought of me. Now I can't say whether she meant she thought of me with the T-shirt, or the card. And although I love the T-shirt, the card totally lit me up. This little act of sweet-kindness gave me an opportunity to feel my own amazingness. We all want our kids-in-law, or our own kids for that matter – to love and see us as Human Beings whom they find something wonderful in, someone they can relate to, or appreciate... but it's not always easy. What is possible is to choose our perspective about whatever happens in interactions with them. And every time I look at her card, which sits on my window sill – I am reminded that *I am a Magical Unicorn.*

Chapter 8:

Showing Up for Yourself

*"We do not believe in ourselves until someone reveals
that deep inside us something is valuable, worth
listening to, worthy of our trust, sacred to our touch.
Once we believe in ourselves, we can risk curiosity,
wonder, spontaneous delight, or any experience that
reveals the human spirit."*
– E.E. Cummings

Welcome to your oasis of rest for your heart. Relax and melt into Essential Element Number Six – Radical Self-Care. While you cozy down, let me set down a little context.

2008 was a particularly difficult year for me in my third marriage. To be fair it was a tough year for many people. With the fall of the market and the collapse of the banking industry, it financially affected many industries and our business was not left out. Offering compassion and understanding to my ex-husband now, it was a very hard time to run our business, a fact I understood even then. Truth is we were both in the storm and at the time, all I needed was to feel valued for the part I played to support us. In any event, the financial environment, notwithstanding, my level of happiness had been failing from long before. It didn't matter how many times I started over, created a new plan or gave up my basic emotional needs, my life in my marriage felt empty and painful. Feeling completely alone and hopeless, I had a stretch of time when not crying became challenging. All I could feel was my sadness.

Looking back now, I feel certain it was grief, because it felt like that unexpected wave that would come over me and move me to weep. I knew that I was at a low, but locked-in by my earnest desire to "make this marriage work", I decided it was time to go back and visit my deeply trusted therapist. A truly gifted psychologist whom I had seen off and on, both with my husband and on my own, since my step-son's passing during the first year of our marriage. After many years of therapy, I felt he truly knew me, appreciated and understood me, believed in me, and cared about me like I was his family. He was like a wonderful, wise, slightly older brother. His genuine caring and skilled counseling comforted me so profoundly that I credit him with saving my mind, and my life.

This year, as I was saying, was rough. I was working at our agency doing human resource work, as well as all the 24-hour work that came home from the office. I wasn't paid a salary. I was the wife who worked in the business. Not being able to let go of my accumulated grip on sadness, I went to see my psychologist doctor. While trying to convey the extent of my despair, I asked him if he could admit me into a hospital. I wanted to go on a medical vacation away from it all. He knew me well enough to know that wasn't the answer. He offered me a fellow psychiatrist's contact info, so that I could receive anti-depressant drugs, if I should continue to believe I needed them. I felt, deep down, that I knew what my problem was and so I talked with him about my deep sense of feeling alone, unappreciated and unseen. I felt unhappy, but I still felt a knowing that eventually I could spring back, and I wasn't ready to give up.

In a moment of utter desperation and sincere desire to feel better, I asked him to do something unusual for me. I asked him to give me a letter that said that I needed a mental leave of absence, so I could rest and recuperate from my condition. So, he wrote out by hand, on his letter head the following note: *"To Whom it May Concern: Chris L_____, needs to take a five-week medical leave, beginning March 3, 2008. A re-evaluation will be conducted at the end of the month ..."* and he signed it. I took the letter and went home and within a few days I felt much better. You see, my friend, I was the human resource manager and co-owner of our business and I didn't need permission to take time off. But what his letter did was validate my feelings, my condition of sadness, and it said to me – *you matter*. He made an "I see You" statement, that I took home for my eyes only, that said someone is taking care of me. And now I had a reminder and solid permission to take care of myself.

I asked for help and got it. I took the idea of caring for myself, to a different level; "radical self-care". The psychological, emotional, and spiritual support I received from that one small act, had a huge and empowering effect on me. I felt better in days. I stayed home for a day or two and returned to my challenging life feeling stronger and better equipped to engage with whatever was to come.

Well, this little lesson on self-love doesn't quite end there. Seven years later, long after my third marriage ended, during my Positive Psychology Coach training classes with Julia Stewart, founder of the School of Coaching Mastery, we were given special homework. Studying the quality of gratitude and the positive psychological effects of it, we were instructed to think of someone who we looked up to, and who had played a particularly special and positive role in our life. Our assignment was to write a letter to them. Explaining what they did, what it meant to us, what it inspired us to feel or do. Then create a gratitude statement to thank them, for their profound contribution to our life. Contact them, arrange to meet (if possible), and to read them our letter of gratitude – face to face.

Now I invite you to practice and experience the benefits in this exercise which are multi-dimensional. You are tasked to look around in your past for someone extraordinary who positively contributed to your life. Angels whose deeds are naturally given through the generosity of their spirit, and who are often overlooked if we aren't already positivity detectives, as we march through the business of life. Angels who under the radar supported you to the success you have now. It could be a teacher who inspired you, a friend who solidly believed in you when you doubted yourself, the checker at the grocery store who is always positive and friendly, or a family member who, from your childhood on, always showed presence with you and celebrated you at every visit.

I hope you can think of many, my lovely friend, but at this selection of *one*, I choose my psychologist. The exercise was, as you can guess, a two-way gift of profound benefit. An opportunity is created for two people to see the spiritual beauty and grace of the other. And to hear and have demonstrated the impact they have on other's lives that they may not have realized. A practice in self-love, self-acceptance, humility and grace-giving. My experience felt like a beautiful communion of souls as we both were filled with gratitude, compassion, loving-kindness, friendship, appreciation and all the other super powers ignited in us, by the power of this expression of gratitude.

Your assignment is to take the time to do the same exercise for your life. Self-love, self-acceptance, humility and grace-giving … all of these are on your RX prescription slip from me. This practice is a beautiful gift to yourself.

Here's a bonus: on my Thank You page, you will find my personal offer to you. A special treat if you accept your self-love assignment. Check it out.

More on TLC (Tender-Loving-Care)

With what I am calling, radical self-care, knowing when, how and in what way to seek or self-administer care is crucial. Mindful attention to yourself must be paid, by you. It can make a tremendous difference in how self-compassionate your healing feels. You have had your heart broken open and your world turned upside down. It's like you dropped into the ICU and when you opened your eyes to take stock of what has happened, the only thing you can feel is pain. And so how you move forward, the steps you choose to take to care for yourself, or request care from others, are important decisions to consider. It is time for *you* to show up for yourself – as your *own best friend*. The rest of this chapter will be ways, or concepts, my dear, to help you to do just that.

Show Up for Yourself

Fact: you are *not* your thoughts. This is a profound statement. Consider this: your beliefs create your thoughts. Your thoughts create your emotions. Your emotions influence your actions. Your actions on the same hamster wheel of habit, become you. Exploring your core beliefs to understand all the "stuff" you have learned, collected, and put into your Being to become who you are, is a very self-loving, liberating, brave, challenging, and transformative process. You don't know what you don't know, about yourself until you get curious. Years of wisdom taught by all walks of higher consciousness teachers, such as Pema Chodron, the Dali Lama, and others, offer their views that, it is the difficulties and challenges that trigger opportunities for us, as we seek relief from pain, which eventually lead us to ignite curiosity about yourselves. Curiosity about what makes us the way we are. What leads us to see the world the way we do. Not everyone is open to the opportunity or sees it when it arrives. So, my dear, I am letting you know your opportunity has arrived.

The painful difficulties of your current state will call out "all hands-on deck!" to your inner critic. All the blame, shame, negative self-views that can be pulled out of all your subconscious' deepest buried beliefs will rise to the surface. Experiences negatively interpreted and internalized creating evidence that now supports your inner critic thoughts that somehow you didn't measure up enough, weren't funny, or smart, or beautiful enough, to keep this event from happening. These may be among the thoughts that flood you during this time, like a do-loop in your mind, that you can't press *stop* on. Negative thoughts triggered by normal things that occur, long after you thought you had put it all to bed.

Here's the self-loving juice, my sweet friend; you are in the perfect place to begin this magical discovery of who *you* are. Ways to begin: Explore mindfulness and what it means and how to practice it. According to Jon Kabat-Zinn the founder of mindfulness-based stress reduction, "Mindfulness is awareness that arises through paying attention, on purpose, in the present moment, non-judgmentally.... It's about knowing what is on your mind." Notice what thoughts are running through your mind, observe them. Write them down. Don't believe them or judge them to be right or wrong. Just practice opening to be aware of them. And with each moment of awareness, plant the seed that you have choice about how to respond or not respond. If you feel painfully triggered, practice Tonglen Meditation to self-lovingly breathe through the moment. Beginning a mindfulness practice is illuminating as you notice the patterns of thoughts that arise on a regular basis. This is great homework to untangle and shift for your beautiful strength and evolution forward. To practice on your own, is completely doable, and can reap surface benefits. However, working with a coach skilled in supporting you to unearth deeper treasures on this path can jump start the process on your way to a life transforming experience.

Let's do a little exploration around one of the beliefs that could be triggered on your path to healing. Let's do a little untangling with the topic of Betrayal. The most straight forward definition to me is: It's the act of disloyalty from someone that you believed to be loyal. As I researched some additional definitions to offer on this topic, regarding the word betrayal, I came across an online dictionary site called Urban Dictionary which caught my eye. As I read their dictionary's definition, I thought, this example demonstrates how anger and grief unprocessed turns into bitterness and has a destructive power to grab your heart and choke it to death. An example of who you might become without authentic healing, seemed, a perfect place to begin this work.

The site is sad and full of pain, which shows the need for compassion and a needed redirect for the energy they have imprisoned themselves with. One of the definitions offered by a wounded Being from the Urban Dictionary is: "Betrayal is when your ... girlfriend decides to make up with/engage in sexual acts with another guy after all the great things you've given, offered, bought, done to her, with the excuse of "wanting to get more experience", thus leaving you with a broken spirit and with a bunch of emotions of hatred, loss of self-respect, and loss of self-confidence, loneliness and total ... sadness." Some of the definitions are darkly humorous, but all of them depict a deep belief that their experience of betrayal proves their worthlessness and validates their sense of unlovability.

What my experience with betrayal has shown me is that, the meaning you give the act of betrayal, is the most important place to focus your attention. It is more a definition of who you believe yourself to be in the exchange in your relationship. Now, stay with me sweetie, it is true you have been betrayed by your most trusted love. And this calls for authentic self-compassion and acknowledgment. You have been deeply wounded. But even in your wounded state, you have power in the choice your make around the "meanings" you give the actions of your husband. And what in turn, you interpret his actions to say about you.

When my guy betrayed me, I found myself wondering if I even knew how to be an adult in relationship. I asked myself, "What does it mean to be an 'adult'?" I explored it with my beautiful, and endlessly gifted mindfulness coach, Melissa. She turned me on to the brilliant Dr. David Richo, author of many books, but the one that truly helped me is *The Five Things We Cannot Change ... and the Happiness We Find by Embracing Them*. One of his "things" is that "People are not loving and loyal all the time." He starts this chapter with a powerful quote from James Hillman: "For we must be clear that to live or love only where one can trust, where there is security and containment, where one cannot be hurt or let down, where what is pledged in words is forever binding, means really to be out of harm's way and so to be out of real life. And it does not matter what is this vessel of trust – analysis, marriage, church, or law, any human relationship."

Wow! Brilliant!

Mr. Hillman had me at hello.

What you learn about human relationships, as you move through the spiritual evolution of opening up to the things that frighten you, is that no one gets through life without being betrayed or hurt by someone. And you don't complete your life without betraying or hurting someone, intentionally or unintentionally. No one escapes. Your spiritual challenge is to learn to be more self-aware, to notice where you are being hurt or feeling betrayed. To understand that you are called to accept all the human responses that come your way. To not use these experiences against yourself to feel bad about, nor to make the other person wrong. But to love your way through it. That is, to be true to your intention to be loving. Now let's be clear: This path to healing will require much work to identify your current boundaries, determine if they are healthy and, if necessary, redesign them to establish healthy boundaries. This task is foundational and must be a top priority.

Staying true to your intention to be loving is not a manifesto for self-sacrifice or permission to self-abuse, or for others to abuse you. It is however, an anchor with which to ground and center your energy so that you can begin to shift your perspective more self-empoweringly and allow your light and brilliance to shine.

There is a beautiful pond of self-loving waters that invite exploration into the concept of Belonging. When you feel you belong, there is a sense of tribal loving protection that can support you through just about anything. I confess, I still struggle at times with not feeling completely understood in the circles I socially engage in. With curiosity and self-compassion, I continue to find inner clues to my own reasons. I sometimes share out loud these feelings, to which, my closest friends argue that I am simply full of bologna sauce. Still it is *my* experience and *my* interpretation, and I will continue to explore it to understanding.

Recently I decided to experiment and intentionally change my mind about my self-interpretation. I decided to accept that I am exactly who I am. And that sometimes I will be comfortable as the party girl, and other times I will attend the party, quiet and reflective. Sometimes I will "yak it up" and other times I will be all ears. Sometimes I will be full of great creative oral stories, full of fun and wisdom, and sometimes I won't even be able to remember everyone's name. But no matter where I am, I will choose to remember that I am amazing. And I will choose to know that no matter who I am in that moment, I belong wherever I am. Because I believe there is a higher force at play and there is a powerful reason – seen or unseen – for me being right where I am. Now it's your turn. Take my experiment and apply it to a place where you want to feel deeper belonging. Remember you are amazing. Just as you are. As I end this chapter I offer you four brief important tips on radical self-care.

Four Radical Care Tips

1. Sharing your story around your heart-breaking event is a powerful consideration. No matter how private you are, you will reach an emotional tipping point where you need to tell someone, if for no other reason but to move the painful energy. Choose wisely. Think about who you know who will non-judgmentally listen and simply love you. Who can hold a sacred space for you that says: I hear your pain; I am here with you. How can I support you? Be sure they can be trusted. The last thing you need is to have that person promise to keep your confidence and then turn and tell. Sometimes your best choice is a therapist, or a coach. And other times, you have a tribe from which, you can choose the best soul of discretion, to hold your confidence, till you are ready to share further. My choices, after much thought, were in this order: my sister (who did the magnificent & much needed "how dare he!" dance for me); my wise, even-handed and pragmatic neighbor

girlfriend (who responded with insightful and powerful questions for me to ponder); my closest girlfriend (who I met years before in my coach training certification program, who speaks my heart's language as my spiritual-sister); and my eons-wiser than her young years, mindfulness coach (who reminds me every time that I am a powerful & wise Being). From there following my period of grief, I shared with my circle of life-long girlfriends. As I began to integrate the experience I had endured and now sought to self-lovingly heal, it began to blend in a life enhancing and transformative way into my everyday life. Healing comes with fierce forgiveness and courageous integration.

2. Ask your husband for whatever self-care support you need. Use your imagination. During the beginning of my healing, it was difficult for me to be physically close to my guy while I felt so disconnected by pain from him. My feelings of emotional separation were more physically painful when lying next to each other to sleep. I found it difficult to get the rest I so deeply needed. I asked him to sleep in the guest room so that I could have space free of the wounded energetic presence I could feel while he was in the room. His willingness to kindly accept my request gave me space to finally rest. This little act of kindness and understanding on his part meant the world to me. My dear, ask for what you need.

3. Hire a coach if you feel so inspired. My coach supported me in a way that contributed significantly to the wide range of personal work I called myself to do.

Geared with intention to invite the unfolding of whatever was to come and to build my self-love and deeper strength without attachment to the outcome. This is a powerful time of healing. Find your woman warrior healing resources and do the work.

4. Watch inspiring movies that tell stories of women who develop personal power and self-love while they journey their challenging and painful experiences. Stories that make you cry with inspiration and laugh at the same time. Check out: *Under the Tuscan Sun, One True Thing, Elizabeth, Moonstruck, Sex and the City....* Just to name a few.

These tips lay a path to our next chapter where we will venture further into concepts and practices that will build your self-love and healing muscles.

Chapter 9:

Your Heart Warrior Bootcamp

"Love is an act of endless forgiveness, a tender look which becomes a habit."
– Peter Ustinov

"You were assigned this mountain to show others it can be moved."
– Anonymous

Forgiveness is an everyday practice. Every single day. Every day it is a renewed commitment. So, let's get familiar with Essential Element Number Seven's circuit – Build New Muscles.

A friend with intimate knowledge of my relationship challenge, and in deep struggle to forgive and let go of the resentment he felt from his partner having tried to commit suicide, asked me, "Have *you* really forgiven him?" With a profound energetic sense of inner peace, I answered, "Yes. I have for-given him. And I forgive him again every day."

In this chapter, you are being called to commit to training everyday as you move toward healing, self-love and self-em-powerment. Moving forward with loving intention to heal in your marriage. This is what your heart is whispering to you that it wants right now. It is a big mountain, but not unclimbable or unmovable. What it will take to reach your love goal, is a commitment to a daily mindful and self-loving practice. A pro-gram to build new muscles over the broad range of your Super Powers which will create the foundation to new ways of being in relationship with your husband, and yourself. And to do the beautiful and courageous work of rebuilding your marriage.

This book covers a variety of *BigLove* muscle building prac-tices to pick from and train with every day. In this love letter to you, I have included lots of inspiring ideas for you to practice with. In one way or another, I have practiced with them all in my personal healing journey, and I will continue to for my life. I live the benefits, so I feel great about suggesting them from experience. In this chapter, I offer you additional key concepts and practices to consider as you explore deeper toward your desired goal. Your goal is a compassionate journey for healing with intention toward creating a recommitted loving relation-ship from here. At this point, it may seem impossible to think of total comfort with trusting again. My dear, trust is possible again. Believe it. Time will tell if your man is genuinely avail-able to be the man worthy of your trust again. Regardless, you will grow in beauty and strength of heart as you develop your essence of love muscles and with that growth, you will have the strength to make decisions – whatever they are. You are wise. You are strong. You are powerful. To make your marriage work you must trust in your trust. It's just like when a moment of happiness shows up, you need to trust your happiness. Take your renewed trust and begin rebuilding your foundation, one love brick at a time.

As you are rebuilding your castle of love, don't be afraid to feel your life again. Let your tears flow whenever you are moved. One day you will find you can talk about this "event" and not feel the need to cry. You will feel a sense of compassion and forgiveness and understanding. You will also feel a new intimacy with your man, who also rose from the ashes of this painful experience. Grief is a process that softens your heart to allow in compassion, love, and forgiveness. A softening process that strengthens your spiritual essence. Take to heart your commitment to train and transform the experience of your marriage and you will be amazed at what becomes possible. The following are more practices to consider. Dive in Love.

Building Love's Muscles

As I mentioned, forgiveness is an everyday program that requires repetition and commitment. It is a steady process that must be engaged in mind, body and spirit everyday if it is to transform your relationship. The results of forgiveness are cumulative in effect. The longer you stay dedicated to the practice the better your results. You practice, feel better, then struggle, fall, get up and start the practice again. All over. A fresh start, doing the best you can every day. Then time passes and one day, months or years later, you notice something is different. You feel different. The heaviness that used to sit on your chest has lifted. You find yourself laughing and seeing your husband through different eyes. Eyes that see the man you love, and you feel somehow free to be happy that you are with him. It feels good. And suddenly you think, "I feel like I have forgiven him." You even have those moments where you think, "I am in-love again." This does not happen all at once, but these moments, one day at a time of healing, collect and add up. And you realize, "Okay. We are good." For this to be possible, a consistent dedication and practice to this goal is essential. Again, dear friend, forgiveness is an every-day muscle to be built up.

As you practice and stay focused, things feel better. Then something happens, and you are tweaked and triggered back to that place that reminds you what you went through. This committed practice, will support you. Those moments when you feel a poke, will become nothing more than reminders that forgiveness it is an everyday practice for all your future, every day. A spiritual and emotional life style. It's a practice of forgiveness, that is not to be infused with resentment, to be complained about, or thrown up in his face, but is to be tended to, with love, over and over, for as long as it takes to completely let go of the past. You may never fully be able to let go but even that, dear love, can be utilized to remind you to love, and what better way is there to value an experience. Your attitude of acceptance, love and willingness to do the work is just as important as the work. So, come from love. Embody love. Practice *BigLove*. This is your whole heart calling each day. I will wish for you that you find, as I did, that this is a truly personally transforming spiritual life path.

You and your husband are starting your marriage over. You are clearing the board and beginning again. So why not create a new beautiful presence with each other? Create a new appreciation and vision of each other and your marriage. Have a love goal. Create an intimate vision of your relationship and what you see for yourselves together. Get creative with how you express your loving regard for each other. Put your effort into it. Once you have gained some strength, invite your husband to imagine yourselves in new love courting stage. What wonderful adventure could you both enjoy with the other? See what comes up. Put in kind effort to understand each other even while you are both struggling to communicate, see it as an invitation to practice new ways to open and soften to each other.

Open to allow inspiration for creative juices to flow in you around tools to work with. I love to communicate and write. While on my healing path, I found myself stuck in one repeated communication practice which always started with best intentions and ended with crying. He and I just couldn't move further. Inspired by my frustration, there came a point where, I insisted we make a list of (what we called) all the "conditions for us staying together" and the "from now-ons" list. These lists served as a place for both of us to have a voice. We clearly defined our in-the-moment emotional boundary. Our line in sand. It represented what was truly important to us, in order to be happy. It wasn't just about me. Or just about him. It was our wants. I truly wanted to know what he wanted. And to identify what would bring each of us happiness. With mindful effort to stay soft, nonjudgmental, no excuses for our wants, accepting and kind, we explored what we wanted and created our list. I remember at the onset, feeling in a mood of irritation, which I chose to breathe through to shift. It was hard. We were at the point where I wanted to holler and stomp, which would have only shut us down again.

So, I chose to surrender to the moment and soften. And I asked my guy to stay soft. Lower our tones. I took responsibility for myself and he followed. I jotted down our requests. Typed them out and posted the Large Font list on our wall. There we could see our agreement – one heart to another – and our intentions for our every day. The "doing" action, the intention and the agreed commitment to stay true to the requests, created a place to start to move from our stuck-ness. It initiated an emotional release of the grip of fear that came to call on our healing path. It allowed more space of ease for what was naturally unfolding. In turn, we eased up on each other, and ourselves. We redirected our energy into other areas of our life that required our attention. We had looked at the pain we were in and chose to create an energetic love contract. Our contract list included simple items like: We promise to watch our tone of voice. We promise to pay better attention to our negativity. We promise to greet each other with sincere presence and interest. And on, and on.

These are not complicated, but these were areas we felt our struggle in, as we moved through our field of wounds still healing, and so we called it out. We choose to believe that we could trust the other to honor them. We held ourselves accountable to do the same. When we noticed a failure to honor, we would point it out to the other. We would point to the list. Sometimes we'd become peeved by it, like getting a foul called on you in a game, and sometimes we would laugh about it and tease each other, but each time we engaged with it brought deeper value. As time when on we turned to the list less and less, it was like we integrated the energy of the list into us. We weren't perfect every day, but we were perfectly imperfect … just as we were.

The list is still posted and now is a caring reminder of our commitment to heal and love each other.

During our path, even with our lists, we communicated with tender and fierce honesty, we accepted that although we were committed to healing and being together, we knew there are no guarantees. So, we trained in getting comfortable with uncertainty, by easing up on our fear of failure for the outcome, dealing with the day to day and staying focused on our goal. We practiced a deeper noticing of the loving effort given by the other.

Practice noticing what your own contribution or detraction from the process is. Ask yourself. Are you practicing with an open-heartedness to whatever comes with an eye on the upside? This level of effort and commitment is what my experience has shown me is required to achieve this loving goal. It is gratifying to recognize that in the larger picture, even the really difficult days, offer something beneficial.

If you believe life is *for* you, then nothing is wasted. From this perspective whatever comes brings you some wisdom to be harvested. With your strength of heart, you can find comfort knowing that if what comes, sucks, then you deal with it authentically, process it, and then get on with your "Yes" to life, using everything you've learned for your growth.

So what about him? My darling, this book has been written to help you achieve what you desire for yourself, and your marriage. An important part of what you desire at this point, includes your man. Your love, your husband. So, let's put a little light on your very important person. It's time to get curious about your husband, about renewing your knowing of him. Like a renewal of your love story. Who is he? Do you know?

Over the years, he has changed too. Have you noticed? What is he noticing about himself? Is he at the stage where he is wondering who he is, what his legacy will be, who will care? He is going through his unique experience as well. He has to heal just like you. If he has accepted ownership of his act of betrayal and is truly devastated by the pain he has caused you, he will be struggling to see himself as someone worthy of your love and trust again. He needs to be able to let his story about himself transform to something self-redeeming. You have to let him, help him, love him. So, get curious. Invite opportunities to share who you now see yourselves as. Ask: How would you describe who you are?

During this exploration aspect, clarify the goal of this task, and try to keep it focused on this new love story goal. Mindfully stay away from the betrayal baggage for now. This practice needs fresh open air to grow and bloom. You can deal with the betrayal details or triggers another time. Stay true to the focus for this practice. As I was saying, go back to the beautiful sparks that began your romantic love beginning and reminisce together. What did you love the most about him? Tell him. Let yourself remember the feeling. Ask him if he remembers the feeling. What do you love the most about him now? Tell him. What do you see as his powers? What does he think his powers are? Notice and appreciate. Allow yourself to recognize where his strengths are and express appreciation for them. Let him into your heart. You have to be brave and open your heart for this to work.

So does he. Let him feel wanted and needed. He has to know that he matters, and that he matters to you, for him to want to stay. If all he sees when he looks at you, or hears in your voice when you speak, or feels when laying next to you in bed is the pain he has caused you and the punishment he thinks he deserves, then he will not be able to live with you or himself. Authentic forgiveness is the only way, for both of you. Love is the only way. Love will allow him to forgive himself. To allow him to feel your forgiveness and to change his story from what he did, to who he authentically has become. The husband you can love again. Then you both open the door to integrate your healing into your marriage and your lives.

Here is a sweet Renewal Practice: Consider this daily; No matter how yesterday's practice went, re-commit to begin again every new day. Each day with each new sunrise there comes a new chance for happiness. And a closer day to forgiveness and healing. Your power is there every morning and you have a chance to begin again. Don't miss the opportunity and the challenge. If every morning you begin with a spark that leads to discontent, then you will build discontentment. However, if you learn to begin your morning with intention for gentle kindness and connection, and then no matter what comes, just ask yourself, "How can I come from Love with this?" When you practice, you begin to build a pattern of kindness and love. You grow what you give attention to. Give attention to what you "want" to grow with your husband. And make sure you ask him what he "wants" to grow with you. Indeed, ask your man to tell you what he loves most about you. And then just listen. I do. And I love what he says. Ask each other lots of great and love blooming questions and then practice listening.

What does Happiness mean and look like to you? In the movie, *Vanilla Sky* Penelope Cruz's character has this beautiful line. "Every passing moment is another chance to turn it around." And for fun I share her other line. "I will see you in another life when we are both cats." It's a quirky and thought-provoking movie. Great discussion sparker.

Your Sacred Temple

Okay, girlfriend, let's take a self-accepting look at your sacred temple. Your beautiful body. It's time to self-lovingly explore your health. Where are you on the spectrum of health? Are you in peri-menopause, menopause, post-menopause? How is that showing up physically, emotionally, mentally in you? If you are experiencing lots of the normal hormonal change challenges, what are you choosing to do to help yourself? What are you choosing to maintain your strength, clarity and sense of emotional and spiritual balance? It all counts.

Proper care of your divine vessel enables you to increase your success in giving your best. If you just ignore your care about these impactful changes, you may as well surrender to the shape-shifter alien take-over, which makes your healing path harder than it already is. The challenges and effects of all stages of menopause, a.k.a., "change of life" are real, and can play a leading energetic part in how it all unfolds. My experience of menopause full range showed me that we can become someone else without realizing it, and we wake-up and ask, "who *is* that speaking out of my mouth?" That's when it might be a good time to research holistic means to come to your rescue.

Explore on topic authors, Susan Somers and Dr. Susan Love and others listed in End Notes regarding Menopause. Take care of yourself. Schedule daily exercise, nourish your divine temple with clean fuel and hydration, get the rest you need. Do all that you need to, to energize and support yourself and to allow your brain to create your best self-empowering and self-loving thoughts.

Take Five or Ten

You are doing great! Let's take it down a little. In any muscle-building program as you know there is the essential rest time. The down-time that allows the work of the training to integrate within your body, mind, and spirit. The rest time is super important. It is the *healing* time. What this rest time consists of is: Put the books down. Relax your attention. Break from the self-improvement classes. Take what you have integrated into yourself and go on vacation. Go on a self-examination vacation. Just BE. See what comes up. One word of caution. This is a two-week vacation. A break-time. Not a six-month sabbatical. The practices that you have learned will stay with you but you must come back to mindfulness training soon, because as my experience demonstrated to me, too long away causes your default paths to organize a coup, and that is moving backward not forward. Take a break then come back refreshed, my friend. Practice is your friend.

A Word About the Kids

Whether your kids are young or adults when this "event" occurs, the kids know something is up. Deciding how to manage this requires mindful loving attention and discussion between you and your husband. Decide how you will live your life during this time in front of your children. Children are highly perceptive and sensitive. They can feel the difference of the energy that is in their home. This is whether you tell them or not. And understand that sometimes if you don't at least tell them that you and daddy are working through something but it's not their fault and everyone is going to be ok, they will live the experience from fear. This can color their ability to trust their future relationships. Your behavior has a ripple. Be mindful of it.

You both must agree and accept how you will behave with each other during this healing. Regardless of whether you are successful with your desired outcome, or if you eventually determine it is healthier, to part, how you relate to each other will help your children heal. Your modeling of this extraordinarily painful and difficult event will color their lives. It's a big responsibility. It's a responsibility of powerful love. *BigLove*. Let them see that mistakes in relationships happen. That love is powerful and that their Father is not perfect, and neither are you. That one thing is solid, you are their Mother, he is their Father and you both love them. Help them understand that this challenge is not their fault. That blame and shame, are not helpful. That you are both committed to resolving your challenge. That relationships, just like other parts of life, from time to time have painful struggles and challenges. How you choose to handle them is what matters for the quality of happiness. You have choice. Teach your kids the value and power of choice. Allow them to see you through your power of self-love and compassion.

Energy Lifts

Here are some energy lifting concepts for you to put in your *BigLove* Tool Box.

   ೞ **Practice positivity.** B. Fredrickson, Ph.D, author of *Positivity*, *LOVE 2.0*, and other books, conducted research that showed, we should "aim for a positivity ratio of at least three to one. This means that for every heart-wrenching negative emotional experience you endure, you need at least three heartfelt positive emotional experiences that uplift you." Positivity increases the opportunity for happiness and healing. My dear, commit to practice optimism and positivity more times then you indulge your negative thoughts. There is no question that it is important to honor wherever (positive or negative) you are and allow your feeling to move. Understand that this allowance needs to be married to the practice of self-awareness. Pay attention to the energetic qualities in your voice. How are you sounding to yourself? How are you sounding to your husband? What is the quality of the message coming from your mind, mouth, heart and body? You communicate on many dimensions. Pay attention to your tone and energy. It will tell you much about what you are feeling but may not have realized yet. As your own best friend stay accountable for honest self-awareness, non-judgmentally. Notice your unconscious interaction patterns with both self-talk and your energy among others. Notice how you talk about life. It all matters. Be a detective who notices the good. When a negative thought pops in (as it will – this is real life), then look for three positives to embrace. It's an easy ratio. It increases your overall level of happiness and it's fun!

ᘓ **Use your mirror of love.** When you look in the mirror for any reason, linger a minute and train with self-accepting openness to see yourself for the beauty you are. Through and through. Choose to trust yourself and your instincts. First you trust yourself then you can trust him. If he breaks your trust, then mindfully and self-lovingly choose how to deal with it. Know that you could not have stopped it. You are not responsible for it, nor are you to blame for it. If, in the end, your marriage ends, choose to accept that there is no shame in discovering there is a better life waiting to be realized. Step into your higher wisdom and know that this is true. As you practice, notice that your image transforms in your own eyes. The light of your essence begins to radiate Self-Love.

ങ **Meditate.** Explore and learn three ways to meditate and do it at least once every day. Tonglen is so powerful for your heart. The practice of intentions for all to be free of suffering and the root of all suffering. The practice to invite in forgiveness. May you forgive and be forgiven, with power from the roots of forgiveness. Make up your own meditation prayer. It is the energy of compassion, love and forgiveness, and the practice to stay open to it, that holds the profound and alchemistic power.

ങ **Practice mindfulness.** Mindfully pay attention without judgment to yourself with whatever comes to you, or through you in your day. Own that you have choice. Do this every day. Every new day.

ങ **Create a sanctuary corner for yourself** in which you put the things that remind you of your intention to heal, forgive and love. Decorate it in your own special spirit of creativity. Let it be the place you go to, to process your thoughts, to journal, to read, to meditate, to weep or just to be reminded by its joy, that you have a vision, which you are committed to, with self- compassion and love.

ભ **Create a self-loving visual**, with the same intention as your sanctuary. Place it so that you see it as your first wake up. Create something that triggers good feelings. Something special that allows whatever it is you want to feel. Happy, connected, calm, joyful, and loved. Place it so that when you open your eyes, it is there to greet you and bring you happiness to begin your morning.

ભ **Explore ways to build your sense of significance and belonging**. Identify and create your tribe. Ignite your curiosity about your feminine powers and inherited skills and gifts. Explore the stories of strong women and find out if their story of power, resilience and love inspires and supports your journey. You would be surprised how much power you have as a glorious woman in your own right. You might be surprised at your gifts and the impact your sharing of your gifts has on the happiness of others. I was. One of my clients said the most powerful thing I did for her while coaching her on her path of forgiveness and healing, was to help her see how special and awesome she is. She had forgotten. Her unique star brilliance had gotten buried under the laundry, professional work, family tasks, care-giving, personal care, and all those things we beauties do for our families and our lives. She needed to feel supported and that she was not crazy to want what others called impossible, to forgive her husband. She needed a sacred space to feel her pain, but also with room for love and hope. She told me, that was what meant the most to her. We can't always see the gift we give others. Look for places to give your gifts and you will begin to realize your sense of belonging.

The Magic of Practice

Google defines Neuroplasticity as "the change in neural pathways and synapses that occurs due to certain factors, like behavior, environment, or neural processes. During such changes, the brain engages in synaptic pruning, deleting the neural connections that are no longer necessary or useful, and strengthening the necessary ones."

Neuroplasticity proves that as we practice self-awareness, noticing our thoughts, feelings or actions and rather than giving way to our default, we mindfully choose a different path. We begin to change our behavior pathways. Every time you choose a different response, you carve out a new pathway of behavior. With repetition, this new pathway of thought, word and deed grooves a little deeper and deeper. You can literally change your behavior default and thought default over time. While in the beginning of change, you generally start off struggling to notice the opportunities. Opportunities that appear for you to mindfully choose positivity or optimism, or to lower your voice to soft words or tones. Soon it seems easier, more natural and you realize you have been developing new pathways. Your new way of being in the world emerges. Then you notice you begin to feel uncomfortable again. Because now you feel uncomfortable each time you notice yourself defaulting back to the old behavior of negativity and sharp paths. It is then that you realize you are different. This "new you" must be maintained just like a beautiful garden. Fertilized, appreciated and groomed. If you go on a trip for too long from the care and attention it requires, it will grow wild and become overgrown with weeds. Tend to your garden; love your garden. It will serve you love in return.

Practice Compassion

Become a detective for opportunities where you can practice compassion. Compassion is a muscle builder of love. Earlier this year, I celebrated my sixty-fifth birthday. It brought Medicare, AARP, new doctors, my maiden name, and license renewal. All time-sensitive tasks to accomplish, in a big-time crunch. At this same time, I was long-distance planning my birthday party in my childhood hometown, with the super-generous help of my high school to lifelong best girlfriends. Suffice it to say, the DMV is always an experience of patience and endurance. On this afternoon, I had arrived for my scheduled appointment. Which turned-out to mean it would only take me four hours to get to the front counter. Ha! What is worth sharing about this day is that little did I know, as I began my four-hour wait, a big invitation to be compassionate would show up on this day.

As I stood in line, I vexed over whether my hair would look okay in the new photo that I would have to "live with" for ten years. My hair and I have been struggling with our relationship for decades. I think I am winning. But that day at the DMV my hair was winning. That day I was tired, hungry and bugged that even with a pre-made appointment I would still have a long stand in line. Didn't anyone know my hair could frizz up with all the human humidity that the packed joint was producing? Being a life committed detective of positivity myself, I kept challenging my mood and looking for the good. I soon entered an interesting conversation with the guy standing next to me, who given his vast physical disabilities, no doubt was having a much harder time standing, than I.

Soon, I was called up. As I explained what I needed to my clerk, I became aware of a lady sitting down at the lower counter to my left and her clerk was rattling off, "you need this ... you need this ... you need this.... Come back when you have it." Wow. Her clerk dropped the forms on the lower counter in front of her. As soon as the clerk turned, this tired, frustrated elderly lady, put her hands up to her face and began to cry. Meanwhile, my clerk was rattling off my requirements too. So, I was trying to listen. Being at the DMV is kinda like the guy in Jerry Seinfeld's *Soup Kitchen Nazi.* I was afraid to tick my clerk off because if she left, you never knew if she would come back. And I didn't want to hear my clerk say "No soup for you. Out!"

So, I paid attention and waited for an opening. The minute I could, I turned to the lady. I didn't want to invade her space or scare her. I didn't know if she was emotionally or mentally unstable and so didn't want to incite her. So, I was very careful. I gently asked if she needed help. She just cried. I could see the papers strewn all over the counter. I told her, if she wanted, I could help her fill out her forms, explain what they meant and help her do what was required. I offered to give her ride home since she was in no condition to take the bus. She just had to wait for me to finish my process. She was so embarrassed about crying, she told me she would wait outside. What struck me deepest was that, while she cried, no one stepped forward to comfort her. Not even the clerks. But right after I did, several people and the clerks all thanked me for reaching out to her. But what if I hadn't been there? I think I was meant to be there. We all have a part to play. Mine was a small act that offered her kindness and compassion and made me feel super wonderful. She turned out to be a fabulously lovely lady with a great story. That day she was a frightened lady recently relocated from the east coast, with no friends, and just needed a friend. As I drove her home and she shared her story, I told her, "Well, now you have one new friend, in your new town." We have remained in touch. My sweet friend, here's a reminder to practice compassion; it feeds your soul. Volunteer your time to help others when you can, it may be just the salve your healing heart needs.

The Cherry on Top

One of the joys of all this training, and is an essential part of the healing, is that it calls attention to remembering to practice having "fun." Seriously. It's easy to lose the sense that you will ever enjoy freedom from the seriousness of your current situation, and just have fun. To laugh till you cry, or wet your pants, or fall down, to feel your lightness with a sense of safe ease might seem all but gone. Have heart, my dear, it is not. It is still there inside you and can be accessed when forgiveness and grace are on the job. Laughter shared between lovers is an elixir to heart-ache on the mend. When it is authentic and can be appreciated for its mutually observed simple and light funny perspective, it is healing. If you and your husband find the same things funny, that is a big plus. If you have to work a little at it, 'cause he has a quirky sense of humor, remember there is always something awesome about everyone. If you look through your love lens, you will see what is there to love. Besides, remember you fell in love with him. Recall what that was about?

Okay my stronger-than-ever, brilliant friend, now that we have moved the mountain with powerful practices, explored and pounded-in the message that forgiveness is an everyday practice, and why all this is *for* you, choose a first step and put it on your calendar of Love. Next, let's move on to the last essential element – appreciation of your heroine's journey.

Chapter 10:
Your Heroine's Journey

"Life is not a rehearsal. It's a practice. Being yourself
is a discipline, a spiritual practice. But you don't need
to listen to whale music, or become a vegetarian,
or chant positive affirmations. You don't need an
ashram. Or a guru. Or a pill. Or an inner goddess or
a shaman. You don't need an MBA or a Ph.D. But the
irony of finding yourself is that you were never lost."
– Caroline McHugh, Never Not A Lovely Moon

D ear heroine, I must confess, before my late fifties, I
was not particularly drawn to identify with concepts
like, heroine, queen, goddess, angel, princess, and
on. I think somewhere in my core I secretly wanted to feel my
sweet femininity, but my childhood was saturated in mascu-
line energy and responsibility, so I never felt the freedom to
express or explore what power these archetypes might hold for
me. I have since come to embrace them as igniters to connect

with Divine Feminism and all the fascinating and diverse ways we can relate to our woman-ness. This brings us to Essential Element Number Eight – Cultivate Self-Awareness. It's time to wake-up the power of your feminine energy and begin to explore its magic.

One thing I have always been sure of, is that I am a never-give-up, true romantic. I wanted to believe in the love story and the idea that love conquers all. Even while my parents' marriage was anything but a fairy tale, I believed my life would somehow end in a beautiful love story for the ages and I would be the heroine. Well, three marriages later, it was time to take a closer look at anything that might shed some light on the things I didn't understand about myself as a divine feminine. I was looking for answers about how to operate this feminine miracle that is me. I started my deep search many years ago, and honestly, I thought I was in good shape, so when my "event" occurred in the middle of what I thought was my sweetest love story, it was time to go deeper. Deeper into the garden of feminine power and this Heroine's journey. Come with me, brave heroine, and let me share the places I looked and the concepts I gathered for strength and what I learned that would be of use to you. Let's start with you.

Who Are You?

Have you ever stopped to process this very big question? Who are you?

I am an essence of love Being, a woman, mother, sister, daughter, grandmother, friend, life-partner, lover, ex-wife, artist, coach, problem-solver, house cleaner, child advocate, seniors advocate, spiritual soul, *BigLove* warrior, singer, dancer, survivor of much, comic, neighbor, magic maker, resilience dancer, goof, and on and on … take a pause and think about who you are and write them down. I bet you will never run out of words to describe yourself once you fall into the space of you. You are a unique constellation of stars – that make one brilliant star – and there will never be anyone like you again. There was never anyone quite like you before. Even identical twins are not identical. You are a star with your own special light, wisdom and essence of love. You may not know it, but you can focus inward and wake up your energy to vibrate your Being, with energy waves that can expand and fill the space of the room you are in. You could argue it is only in our heads or our imagination, but *is* it?

When you begin to study higher consciousness, one of the basics is learning about chakras. The best book according to beautiful Reiki practitioners I have admired is *Wheels of Life* by Anodea Judith, Ph.D. As a way to introduce you to the value of understanding chakras, I want to share some of Dr. Judith's description of our first chakra. Our Root Chakra is *Muladhara*. It is a Sanskrit name meaning "root support". It is of crucial importance. She says, "It relates to the element earth, and all solid, earthly things, such as our bodies, our health, our survival, our material and monetary existence, and our ability to focus and manifest our needs. It is the manifestation of consciousness in its final form; solid and tangible. It is our need to stay alive and be healthy, and the acceptance of limitation and discipline so crucial to manifestation." She goes on, "The purpose of this chakra is to solidify this ground. If we do not balance this chakra before we progress to others, our growth will be without roots, ungrounded, and will lack the stability necessary for true growth." We have seven chakras in our Being of energy. Each one serves a purpose. This was amazing for me to discover. I hope you will be inspired to find out more about chakras for yourself if this resonates for you. That will be your decision, my dear.

What my heart wants you most to get from this is that you are a powerful being and there is a path to learn how to tap into your powers and engage them for your best life. What comes up for you, when you read the description of the first chakra? Reflect on it and journal around it. It could be the start of something amazing for you.

You might be wondering how did this help me on my path to healing? Well, when I felt that I was truly running out of "head" answers, such as logical, reasonable, strategic solutions to resolve my pain; when all the answers "out there" seemed too weak to deal with what I was desperately wanting to find peace with, my coach brought root chakras, back to the front of my mind. I had taken Reiki training and studied chakras at that time, but as is life, so many things had gotten in front of my ongoing study and soon my brain's real estate was filled up with only what was most urgently on my mind. With this reminder, I went back to review and brush up on what I had learned. This is when my lights went on. Remembering my internal forces of higher consciousness and the personal power I felt, ignited my rockets. I felt my energy expand.

My friend, again, this might sound "woo-woo", but it is not just a fairy tale. It is truth. You are more powerful than you know. So, get to know who you are and find out what powerful worlds you can discover and booster rockets you can ignite. You are on a heroine's journey for sure.

A few more thoughts. The process to healing requires you to be brave and stay strong. Think of the practice of forgiveness as a "fail-forward" practice. Train in the moment. Even when you think you aren't doing well, your *willingness to forgive* makes you fabulous.

Practice this Mantra: Notice/Shift/Recommit. Make-up your own little reminder statement. One day I was so discouraged I kept noticing myself thinking back and getting stuck on the things that would come up, finding myself tying them to the past or the future. I was one big heap of monkey brains gone mad. I sat down and I wrote on a bright yellow 8 ½ x 11 sheet of paper in red ink, centered down the middle:

Note to Self

* NOW *

The most important moment is right now.

The present. The past is done – gone.

The future is unknown … ahead.

So today – right now – this moment … then the next …

and the next …

Be the Best YOU – You Can Be.

I signed the bottom with my name, drew a red heart, and posted it on my wall above my desk. It is still posted on my wall. It serves to remind me to ground my energy and believe in my powers of love and compassion. I invite you to find ways to ground yourself. Post this or any message to yourself of your own design for your power and support. Do something powerful and positive for *you*.

You are a warrior woman and on this path, you have an opportunity every day to practice. Make a sweet game of it. Find ways to support yourself and build your self-acceptance and confidence.

During the writing of this love letter to you, I experienced night dreams where I was flying. I have dreamt of flying before by not several nights in a row, and not with such an easy take off. Now to be clear I am speaking of a dream where I can fly. I simply lift off and fly. One night I was flying with my sister, one night with some of my girlfriends. It was quite amazing. I am good at remembering my dreams and I have some doozies. But these dreams were amazing in that I had had dreams weeks earlier where I was being squished in little rooms and the floors were moving and there were lots of people I didn't know crammed in. Anxiety dreams I am sure. To shift to dreams of flying was a very wonderful event. What I took from that is that my powers of self-confidence had finally ignited. I had felt concerned about writing this letter to you, I wanted it to be what you needed to support you and help you wake-up to who you are with all your glorious power. I can't be sure, but I want to say my flying dreams were trying to tell me to believe.

Simply believe. Well, I do.

I believe in *you*.

My wish for you is to have dreams of flying of your own, and to come to know that you are powerful enough to soar.

One last delicious point. My perspective about the hopeless romantic. I remember that one of the biggest disappointments my heart was feeling with my "event," was that I felt I would have to give up on my written-in-stone, tattooed on my heart, commitment to romance. I was so angry that my guy had taken that away from me. I feared I would consider all romantic movies with a cynical bitterness, and I wouldn't be able to appreciate and fall into romantic stories. Essentially, I would never be me again. Well, that fear stayed with me for a while.

Even so far as to make it impossible to watch my own romantic videos of my guy and I, videos that used to warm my heart. During my dark grieving time, I couldn't watch them without triggering irritated grief and anger. I felt the distraction of wondering what might have been going on covertly at that time, on the way to my guy breaking my heart. Seriously. Yes, you can hear I was creating more suffering for myself.

As I worked the same path I am offering you now, with this love letter, my friend, I soon was able to engage in love stories and my own sweetie videos again without the suffering. I was freed to watch them with sweet energy, romantic love energy, and hope. I decided to change the tag I gave myself – from hopeless romantic to *hopeful romantic*. The ending scene of *Shakespeare In Love* (which you can view online) is a hopeful and romantic final scene. Viola is his heroine, and Shakespeare writes, "her soul is greater than the ocean, her spirit is stronger than the sea's embrace." Beautiful.

You see?

Hopeful romantic.

My dear, dear friend, you have traveled with me through my eight essential elements on the path to healing your beautiful heart, life and marriage. I am so grateful, and I send a big hug and kiss to you right now.

I want you to go out and be … the queen, princess, goddess, love warrior, divine wisdom, spirit woman warrior, lioness, wisdom wolf … and heroine in your life. Welcome home whatever brings you sparks of inspiration, to answer the divine invitation to wake-up, meet, and finally begin to know *yourself.*

As we wrap up my love fest with you, I want to leave you some reminders. Just in case you should hit some obstacles along your path. Sprinkled throughout the previous chapters, I've included tricks to overcome several obstacles, but only time will show you what rises as your most challenging triggers. In Chapter 11, I offer more tips to work with to overcome obstacles on your path to healing. Remember obstacles are nothing but invitations with opportunity to practice.

Chapter 11:

Invitations for Practice

"You didn't come this far to only come this far".
— Compete Every Day (Website)

Dear lovely,

The above quote is so right. You haven't come all this way to just get stuck in first gear. Here are suggestions for some of the most common challenges that can hook you on your road to healing.

cs **The "What If" Game.** The what if game goes something like this: What if he cheats again? What if he thinks that since I forgave him he can do it again? What if he acts like everything is normal and I am still upset? What if I think I notice something suspicious? What if I am never happy again? Suggestion: Playing the "What If game" is a game that just increases your suffering. You can't know what he will do. Practice adjusting your perspective. In the end if you get stuck in the

What If game after reading my book, begin reading it again. And I would love to hear from you.

ᦲ **Anxiety about looking back**. Want to look forward but feel stuck with triggers? Suggestion: Looking back and feeling anxiety can be helped by going back to look at grieving. Until you work through the past and complete your grieving you will always be vulnerable to getting stuck.

ᦲ **Your husband won't apologize**. Suggestion: In the end, you must work on yourself first. Once you have built your muscles you will know what to do.

ᦲ **Family counseling isn't enough**. Suggestions: If you have already worked with a therapist and want more assistance on your path to healing, hire a relationship coach. A coach will help you sort out what is blocking the forward movement to forgiveness.

ᦲ **You are afraid to lose him**. Suggestions: Building you own muscles will help you let go of the fear and embrace your own strength. Insecurity and lack of self-love contribute to fear. You can't heal anything with the energy of fear. Working on your relationship with yourself and fear is the first place to start.

ᦲ **Getting stuck in mad**. Suggestion: Seek to accept that healing requires willingness to forgive. Explore where the anger is, how it is and is not serving you, and practice ways to release it. Planting yourself in punishing him or yourself will only block healing. Transforming anger while processing grief is essential.

ᦲ **Resistance to build your self-awareness**. Suggestion: Lack of cultivating self-awareness while putting all responsibility on him to fix the situation and pay-up on the emotional debt will only block healing. Work on your self-awareness development. Your personal growth is key to shift your view and clear your capacity to move forward toward openness and healing.

- ✄ **Seeing him as "bad" and you as "good" – perspective**. Suggestion: Explore what this view brings you and what it prevents you from gaining. Practice shifting your perspective to come from love. Staying stuck in this view will only block your healing.
- ✄ **You see triggers everywhere**. Suggestions: Work with a coach or therapist to help you untangle your hooks and "de-charge" them.

My dear, the work is yours to do. Who you become allows you to bravely see the truth about your relationship and about him for you. Don't wait to be scared alive. You won't change him. You will evolve and grow. He must do the same, if he chooses. Both of you have choice. Do the work, then you can explore what exists with which to create a healthy loving marriage; for the marriage you both want.

The above are some of the places on this path you might get hooked or stuck. Don't give up at the first challenge. The tips in this love letter, throughout each chapter, will give you a good beginning. If you find you need additional help reaching out for coaching or therapy is a great option.

Brave spirit, I have walked this journey that you are now on. I have been where you are. *If your desire is to be supported and experience a deeper dimension of TLC, to evolve compassionately supported by life training and wisdom, I would be delighted to hop on a call to explore the magic we could create together for your most empowered life.*

The life skills of this book can be applied in any number of ways for you or someone you know, who may have been burned by betrayed or wounded in their life. Finding the freedom to forgive is life enhancing and frees you to live an authentically happy life. The application is broad and profound for your whole life. I invite you to share my healing message with others.

Remember you have everything you need to walk this path successfully. However, you are not an island and you don't have to do it alone, my experience has shown, having someone to walk this journey with transforms it to a much more beautiful, loving, and satisfying experience. I would love to hear from you.

Chapter 12:

Once Upon A Time to Begin Again

"Keep the Faith. The most amazing things in life tend to happen right at the moment you're about to give up."
– Unknown

Well, dear friend, you are on the road with a plan for something extraordinary and courageously loving. I believe in you. The concepts and practices that I have offered you on your road to healing, can work. *The most important ingredient is your willingness to forgive.* You can't control what your husband does or does not do. All you can do is to follow the steps offered in this love letter and design a plan to empower yourself to forgiveness. The rest will unfold and working with what comes is part of the growth.

We started your journey connecting with where you are right now. Then I shared my story in chapter two. It's time now to review the key points of each of my Eight Essential Elements for Forgiveness.

Element Number One – Grace of Grief. It is so essential to grieve the loss of trust and safety that has occurred. Your heart has been broken. Grace is the healing power that you ignite within compassion and grief. Grief has a path, and when you honor yourself with mindful and tender self-care, you lay the foundation for genuine and self-empowering healing.

Element Number Two – Love – *BigLove* is the concept that I introduced to capture the wide range of love powers present for you on the road to healing. Their power is vast – and essentially needed for the really big challenges of your new relationship and new life.

Element Number Three – Fierce Forgiveness. This is the golden path. To forgive is essential if your goal is to stay in your marriage and begin again. We explored the process of forgiveness. Now you understand most of all it is an everyday practice and the willingness to forgive is key. As well, should the acceptance of separate lives become your healthiest path, forgiveness remains essential for your future happiness and peace.

Element Number Four – Super Powers. In this chapter, we highlighted the powers you have that you may not be aware of. Your powers aid you on the path to forgiveness and healing. So it's vital, especially now, to appreciate and ignite their beneficial qualities and energy for your relationship and your life.

Element Number Five – Perspective. In this chapter, we explored the magical capacity available to you, with how you view events. How your choice of perspective will assist you in the healing of your marriage and life.

Element Number Six – Radical Self-Care. In this chapter, we explored all the practices that will bring essential

TLC to your heart while you work on grieving and healing to move forward.

Element Number Seven – Building New Muscles. In this chapter, we reinforced the point that forgiveness is an everyday practice. That science now supports with studies, that you can change your mind and ways of being with repeated mindful choice. You were also presented with a number of practices to build resilience and reinforce your love muscles.

Element Number Eight – Cultivate Self-Awareness. In this chapter, we explored ways to wake up to the feminine power that is in you. We dipped a toe in chakras and put out an invitation to get curious and learn more about yourself.

Each of the chapters offered tools and practices to support you on your journey to healing and forgiveness. They only work if you work them. So be good to yourself and take what resonates for you and work it.

This book is designed for the brilliant woman who wants to heal in her marriage after betrayal. This book is a gift to all beautiful hearts who have experienced the pain of betrayal and desire to heal their broken heart as well. Forgiveness is the power of love in action. It's *BigLove*. In order to forgive it is essential for you to begin with a *willingness* to forgive in your heart. Forgiveness is your super power for happiness in your life. Keep that in mind as you practice. Practice well.

My wish for you, beautiful lady, is that your wish comes true. I wish for you to build muscles to support yourself while you practice every day to forgive and heal. My wish for your marriage is that the journey transforms pain into grace and the power of forgiveness heals. That your marriage becomes all it can be; compassionate, loving, and strong and more.

Your Next Step

What is your next step? My dear, choose a practice that you want to begin with. Perhaps you would begin in grief; then simply progress to self-love and practice. You have run the gauntlet in the oven of emotional pain. Still you are brave and powerful – and you can resiliently heal and be happy anew. Forgiveness and Love is what it takes. They are the elixir you seek.

I have included some *free offers,* on my Thank You page, so my deserving friend, choose one and use the contact information to reach out if you are inspired to do so. I would love to hear from you.

I am so grateful for your time in reading my book. I believe there is a higher power at work at all times, and I am grateful that you found me and my message found you. I deeply appreciate you and my hope is that in my love letter to you, you found some really juicy value for yourself.

Two extra gifts. Before you go I invite you to let my original tender piece, a love poem, which I wrote in 2008 – inspire your heart for healing. Written from my romantic spirit but never published, I discovered it in my journal as I was creating this love letter for you. And I thought of you. Following my poem, is my version of a special parable close to my heart, that I want to leave you with. I hope both pieces warm your heart with faith, hope, and love. *BigLove.* Your path to healing is in your hands. What are you willing to learn and practice on the path to forgive and heal in and for your marriage … for your life?

I wish you the stars.

Always from love,
XO Christine

Missing You – A Poem

by C.E. Leon, 2008

Once upon a time, every time you looked at me, you would smile; not a standard smiley face smile, but a smile just for me. One that could melt a glacier the size of Mars. One that lit me up with the feeling – " I'm in love with this guy" – over and over.

Once upon a time, you would stand close to me, close enough to reach out and touch me; which you would do repeatedly, as though you really wanted to feel me, to connect with me, as you told me stories of your day, or charmed me with your new-to-me old corny vaudeville-like jokes, and I would laugh freely, and unburdened by the heaviness of a rough past, not yet lived with you.

Once upon a time, you looked forward to the chance to talk to me, and you joyfully found silly, warm, and endearingly funny things to say to me – mesmerizing me with the wonderful strength and warm resonance of your voice, which would travel through my core's internal network right to the place that tingled with desire for closeness with your place that tingled with desire for me.

Once upon a time, you took my calls when you were at work, no matter how busy you were, and always told me there was no one more important to talk to than me, even when you really needed to go, cause you were honestly busy; and even your secretary knew my significance to you; and to put my calls through and to hold your "other less important" calls, when I called.

Once upon a time, you searched for interesting things to talk to me about in your intimate "I know you" charming tone; topics other than work or baseball or general topics you could talk to the butcher about in your "I'm talking to the butcher" general acquaintance friendly tone. You would watch to see if I was entertained because you wanted to talk to me about things you thought I wanted to talk about even if I didn't – you loved to put the effort there – and bring me into your world.

Once upon a time, you looked into my eyes, at my face, at me and held me in that look – connecting in the moment – with your lovely sky-blue eyes – as though you actually saw me, you held me tenderly with your eyes, I felt cherished by you. And when you kissed me, you kissed me. You meant it. Your kiss was meant for me. Kissing me was what you wanted, and you took each moment, to be in the moment with me. You owned those luscious fully engaged lips that sought to embrace and taste mine; hungrily, tenderly or playfully – always interested.

Once upon a time, you told me that you believed that kindness was the most important quality in any relationship. "Just be nice", you would say. You would pull out, hold, and scoot in my chair for me, open doors for me, walk with me, and look for ways to make me smile in response to you. When you spoke to me, you were sweet, kind and gentle, yes, that is how you were with me.

Once upon a time, we cherished each other.

The time that was once upon, was long ago, at the starry-eyed entry, into what became a long lasting committed relationship that has lived through joy, laughter, love, blessings, fear, loss, tears, anger, detachment, denial, engagement, battle hurt, resentment, achievement, hard, hard work, forgiveness and always the desire to run – married to the desire to start fresh. This is marriage and all the once upon a times that don't happen anymore remain accountable to two, not one, in any marriage.

Once upon a time instead of being angry with you, I missed you and all the once upon a times we had when we were new and in-love.

Once upon a time, now just in time, twenty years later, the once upon a times can begin today.

Are we different? Yes, but a marriage richer, deeper, and more intimate is possible.

Today I realized … I miss you.

As my sweet innocent five-year-old son once wrote on a tiny yellow post-it for me…. Kiss, Face, Love….

Once upon a now … I say to you … Kiss, Face, Love.

A Little Parable for You

One day I was walking in a field looking up at the blue sky and I suddenly fell into a deep hole in the ground. The walls were high and steep and try as I might, I couldn't climb out. I called out for help over and over until finally a holy man came by and stopped. He peeked down and asked if he could help me. I called up "I can't get out can you help me?" He leaned over and sprinkled holy water over me, said a prayer, and offered a blessing. Then walked on. A little later a psychiatrist heard my cries from the hole and stopped to peek down.

"Are you alright?" he inquired.

"I've fallen in this hole and I can't get out," I answered.

He paused and postulated, "Perhaps you only think you're in a hole?" Then he reached into his pocket, pulled out a pad and scribbled something on the paper. He dropped the prescription into the hole and walked on.

By now, I am thinking I will never get out of this hole. As the sun began to drop-low, I continued to cry out for help. A while later, a little woman walked up and peeked down into the dark hole.

She called out, "Is someone down there?"

Quickly I said, "Yes, I fell in and I can't find my way out."

Suddenly she jumped into the hole with me. Flabbergasted I watched her as she got up and brushed herself off.

"Why did you do that?" I asked incredulously.

"Oh!" she said energetically, "I've been here before and I know the way out."

Remember, I have *actually* been here before and I can help you find your way out.

Wishing you tons of love & light.

Christine

End Notes and References

Books Referenced:

Victor Frankl – *Man's Search for Meaning*

Thich Nhat Hanh – *Teachings on Love*

Pema Chodron – *How to Meditate*

https://binged.it/2NTVPYx (Link to Pema Chodron Guided
    Tonglen Meditation)

Rainer M. Rilke – *Letters to a Young Poet*

Michael A. Singer – *the untethered soul: the journey beyond
    yourself*

Lynn McTaggart – *The Field*

Drs. Jett Psaris and Marlena S. Lyons – *Undefended Love*

Nelson Mandela – *Mandela*

Susan Sommers – *Ageless*

Dr. Susan Love's – *Menopause & Hormones*

Dr. Ricki Pollycove, M.D., M.S. – *Bioidentical Hormones*

Dr. Barbara Fredrickson, Ph.D. – *Love 2.0: PositivityReso-
    nance*

Dr. Anodea Judith, Ph.D. – *The Wheels of Life*
Dr. Richo – *The Five Things We Cannot Change*
Jon Kabat-Zinn – *Wherever You Go There You Are*
Urban Dictionary On-Line - https://www.urbandictionary.com

Movies Referenced to Inspire: (google them)
The Abyss - 1989
Cocoon - 1985
Sex and the City - 2010
Moonstruck - 1987
Vanilla Sky - 2001
Wizard of Oz (Glinda Quote) - 1939
Shakespeare in Love - 1998
Life of Pi - 2012
Unfaithful - 2002
The Help - 2011
Under the Tuscan Sun - 2003
One True Thing - 1998
The Green Mile - 1999
Elizabeth - 1998

Television and Video Clips Referenced to Illustrate:
Star Trek – Episode "The Empath"- 1968
Queen Jill Scott – Queendom Quote - https://youtu.be/Cr-lRf-bxzYA
Original Parable can be found at – www.westwing.bewarne.com/queries/story.html

Songs to Pair with this Book:
Pharrell Williams – Happy Song

Alanis Morissette – Torch;

Flavors of Entanglement; Ironic

Lady Gaga – Million Reasons

Adele – Someone Like You

Stevie Nicks – Landslide

Sara Bareilles – Brave; Gravity

Christina Perri – A Thousand Years; Human

Bryan Adams – Everything I do.

Snow Patrol – Chasing Cars.

Sade – Soldier of Love

(Just to name a few)

Acknowledgments

Isn't it sweetly divine when you reflect and realize that the most painful events can create a basket full of silver and gold-linings to enhance your life – if you can keep your eyes and heart open. My life-long friends consider me a resilience wonder warrior. They have witnessed my journey. The resilience they see in me, is what my writing of this magical book required of me, in order to complete. Nothing less.

The writing of this book was a labor of love and healing. No one chooses these hard "events" but when they come making lemonade and sweet cakes is worlds better than drinking poison. My resilience first comes from my choice to trust my strength, and to choose to train to be my best self every day. Next my strength comes from my beautiful, inspiring and loving global tribe of friends and family – all special angels who bring their super powers to support me through thick and thin.

I would love to write the name of every beautiful being I know who has given to my life but that would be a series of books in itself. So – to all of you, yes, You – whom I have ever hugged I Thank You. Thank You for giving me a dose of your love energy whether I needed it or not. One of my favorite parts of visiting anyone is the start and finish where I say, "hugs for everyone!" Which I collect when I arrive and when I leave. Try it. It is Heaven.

A very special ton of gratitude to my amazing guy. Who gracefully and generously helped me dig up the painful past of our event and walked through it again with me – in my effort to step fully back into that first devastating day. As I wrote chapters offering us up in the nakedness of our life event, with intention to serve others, he not only supported me emotionally, but he was patient, kind, and caring. He fed me. He welcomed me to read my raw chapters to him, and he supported me wholeheartedly with his brilliant editorial talent in my eleventh hour. I am so grateful for his love and presence in my life. He is a great soul of courage and strength. And I am deeply grateful that we could heal our hearts so that I could have this story to tell with him rather than without him. I am grateful for our little ones on our adventure still to come. We will make something beautiful of all this - as life unfolds.

I am grateful to my sons, Josh and Lucas, who live their life's with curiosity, passion and fierce strength of character which they cultivated even with the challenges of their childhood with me. You are my Kiss, Face, Love boys. To my daughters-in-law, Jessica and Stephanie, who each shine their special brilliant light. And my grandson, Archer who is nothing but joy in my life. Each of you inspire me.

I am grateful for my two North Stars. My spiritual sister best friend, Lisa, who is my spirit juice and light when I walk through too much dark. My brilliant coach Melissa who helps me remember how awesome and fiercely brilliant I am cause that's how she sees me. This book would have been much harder to write without you both.

I am grateful to my sister Bobbi who let me share our story of love and healing. And who traveled to my home, to help take care of Lizzie, so I could make my writing deadlines. You have my back. You are my fiercest and funniest friend, Sis. You are Love.

To my sister Patsy, my brothers Tim and Rick, I am grateful for our shared lives, and all the opportunities you bring me to practice forgiveness, joy, gratitude and BigLove.

I am grateful to my high school posse of best lifelong friends who have loved me, supported me, cheered for me and been there for me. Who have consistently given me a sense of belonging since we were 16. You're the Best. Patrice, Marlene, Pauline, Linda, MaryPat, Renee, Sue, and Paula.

I am grateful to my enduring tribe of friends who through the years and distance have supported me with their friendship which I carry in my heart. Ginger, Maureen, Robynne, Donna, Dominic, Liz, Susie, Lynn.

I am so grateful to my courageous and gorgeous clients and dear friends, I see and love you, who trusted me and allowed me to use the core of their stories to illustrate concepts and to identify what topics would be most helpful to bring to my book for nuggets of growth in this "event". You are beautiful brave women. You inspire me.

To my parents, Bob and Esther, barbequing in Heaven who without, I might not have looked so closely at what life is all about. You told me "you can do and be anything you want. Just don't leave the front yard." Which I have reframed as:

Turn around and look inside yourself and you will find you are already Home. I missed not being able to read my chapters to you. Love and miss you.

To my quasi-in-laws, Al and Lily, now dancing in the ball-rooms of Heaven – I am so grateful for you both and that you gave me sweet unconditional parental love for almost eight years. Love and miss you.

I am grateful to my ex-husbands who each brought some-thing important, life-changing, and new for me to learn on my journey. B.R. for your good heart and helping me create our sons. Mr. Baseball for giving the best you had every day. I am forever grateful.

I am profoundly grateful to my psychologist and friend, Sonny, who showed me what it felt like to be supported and seen.

Finally, I want to thank everyone – you know who you are – who expressed joy and excitement that I was writing a book. I have been writing for a long time but not publishing. This is my first. It's an amazing ride.

To the Morgan James Publishing team: Special thanks to David Hancock, CEO & Founder for believing in me and my message. To my Author Relations Manager, Gayle West, thanks for making the process seamless and easy. Many more thanks to everyone else, but especially Jim Howard, Bethany Marshall, and Nickcole Watkins.

Tons of Gratitude to Angela Lauria, founder of The Author Incubator for coming across my radar at the not best time but grabbing my heart all the same and opening the door for me to write this book. Expertly leading me to completion with your brilliant author's program. I am grateful for the A.I. Team (Cheyenne, Ora, and Moriah) and the whole Team - who supported me. Generously nurturing and mindfully inspiring me, giving me freedom to shine my light.

I am forever grateful for this magnificent self-empowering experience. I am a Life Coach. I am a writer. And now I am a published Author. I am blessed.

About the Author

Christine has been a certified Life & Relationship (& Transition) Coach, CPC, iPEC, and an ICF member since 2013. Additionally, for more than 20 years she served as a human resource manager, business partner, and remains a co-owner of an insurance agency in the bay area. Her 40th birthday marked her leap into the study of human psychology, fueled by her enthusiastic interest in efficacy (beneficial change) & understanding of herself and others. With sons still in high school, Christine returned to college and graduated from Skyline Community College with an associate degree with honors, with focused extensive studies in psychology in 2003.

In 2012, inspired by her own experiences and the self-discovery of her "true calling" to be of service with empowering contribution to facilitate others' "best" possible life experience, Christine returned with a "student's mind" and began coach training with the institute CTI. Then continued coach training with iPEC and in 2013 graduated with certification.

Continuing to study in 2014 & 2015 – she trained as a practitioner in Reiki (energy healing). She has completed certificate programs in positive psychology coaching, energy & emotional intelligence, the neuroscience of coaching, EFT (Tapping), meditation, and mindfulness. In January 2018, her passion to continue learning and evolve, personally and professionally, inspired Christine to dive into a two-year Positive Psychology Coaching program with Julia Stewart's – School of Coaching Mastery.

In addition to her training and inherent talents – today 65, Christine has life credibility from experience to have practical wisdom and practical understanding in the areas of domestic & substance abuse, illness (chronic fatigue, panic attacks, cancer), depression, parenting (bio & step & foster), marriage, single-parenting, divorce, remarriage, long distance relationship skills, PTSD, multi-dimensional grief recovery, personal growth, and healing through integration.

Christine's is in her flow when she is coaching and inspiring other women while helping and uplifting them to discover their own power and beauty – where they are... to thrive.

Christine currently lives in Santa Cruz County. She nurtures a loving authentic relationship with her beloved life-partner and the blessings of their blended families. They delight in their sweet blonde Beagle – Lizzie Lulu.

Christine creatively expresses through writing, painting, storytelling, photography, singing, dancing, and laughing at the top of her lungs with friends and family. Mindfully and fully connecting everywhere she can to bring her best engaged energy into the unlimited magical possibilities of Life.

Website: https://christineleoncoaching.com

Email: chris@christineleon.coach

Or simply enter: rootsofforgiveness.com to find me.

Thank You!

Beauty, I want to express my most genuine gratitude to you for reading my Letter of Love to you. My gift is meant for you if your heart called you to it. If just one thing I shared, or one question I asked, or one sparkle of love sent to you through my words – landed and is helping to support your courageous heart – then I have fulfilled my wish. Thank you for sharing the time in your life to read my heart-words sent to you. Again, I send tons of Light & Love...*BigLove*. XO

Thank You Gifts:

This journey to healing is very much enhanced through journaling. Almost every chapter invites you to journal. So, to encourage you to find your nuggets of gold in writing down your thoughts, and moving your energy, I created a special Journaling offer. Additionally, in Chapter 8 on Radical Self-Care, a focus on Self-Love, I told the story of My Gratitude Assignment. I'd like to encourage you to get a little Gratitude energy going for yourself, so I have created a special offer for that too.

Look below for my invitations.

Finally, I extend a welcoming invitation to visit my website at https://christineleoncoaching.com

Big Hug.

FREE JOURNAL CALL:

Here for you is a FREE 30-minute video call (face-to-face) or a straight voice call (your choice) – where we will explore one of your journal entries to see what gold nuggets are there for You. To get the Free Journal Exploration Call – Email me at chris@christineleon.coach. Include your email address and attach a copy of your one journal entry page that you wish to explore during the call. Tell me a little bit about yourself. I will contact you to set up our time.

FREE GRATITUDE ASSIGNMENT CALL:

Here for you is a FREE 30-minute video call (face-to-face) or, a straight voice call (your choice) – where we will explore your Gratitude letter and the experience of your face-to-face *BigLove* moment. You will have an opportunity to process the special healing juice that came up for you - with me. To get the Free Gratitude Assignment Call – Email me at chris@christineleon.coach . Include your email address, attach a copy of your letter and a little about yourself. I will contact you to set up our time.

"What if you woke up today with only the things you thanked God for yesterday."

A Gratitude Meme

May you be free of suffering and the root of all suffering.

May you be filled with forgiveness and the root of all forgiveness.

May you be filled with abundant love and the root of all abundant love.

Wishing you love,

The Beginning.

Christine

Printed in the USA
CPSIA information can be obtained
at www.ICGtesting.com
JSHW021344180724
66662JS00002B/93